BUYING OUT THE BOSS

THE SUCCESSOR'S GUIDE
TO SUCCESSION PLANNING

BUYING OUT
THE BOSS

MICHAEL VANN
and
KEVIN VANN

LIONCREST
PUBLISHING

BUYING OUT THE BOSS

The Successor's Guide to Succession Planning

ISBN   978-1-5445-1130-6 *Paperback*
      978-1-5445-1131-3 *Ebook*

This book is dedicated to those family members who have come before us and laid the foundation for the Vann Group and to those who have come to rely on our advice and planning over the years. We thank our families, friends, partners, associates, and certainly our clients for all of the support they've given us. To the next generation of Vann Family members, we hope some of you will get a chance to buy out the bosses!

CONTENTS

FOREWORD

BY TODD MARION

Our company hired Kevin and Michael Vann of the Vann Group based on some referrals from other successful family businesses in the area, who all swore by their expertise in planning, problem-solving, and general advisory services. Our family business included three uncles who were nearing or at retirement age and six cousins who had various levels of responsibility within the organization. I had reached the level of CEO.

Over many years, I had watched our company attempt several times to come up with a succession plan that would satisfy both the retiring uncles (one of whom was my dad) as well as all the cousins in the business with us. Additionally, there were nonoperating family members—spouses, nieces, nephews, and other cousins—who also had at least a minimal interest in seeing the company transition successfully to the second generation.

We had hired consultants, advisors, and attorneys over the years, asking them to come up with a plan that would not only satisfy each family member but also make financial sense for the company. Each time, we would get close to an understanding, but then challenges would arise both on the personal and business level. The plans and the planners would be put on the shelf. This went on for eight years without resolution.

When I discussed with Kevin and Mike the history of the failed succession planning, they told me to be prepared to stay 100 percent focused on what's best for the company first. Then we would see if the stakeholders will fall into place. We have always been a very close-knit family with a one-for-all-and-all-for-one work ethic and sense of belonging. It was painful to watch some of the family reactions as the Vanns took on each business and personal challenge and stumbling block.

I watched the process unfold. I saw them painstakingly put their own credibility, advice, and personal relationships at risk with each family member, persisting until the pathway was cleared of challenges. The process took three years. There were times when I thought the Vanns would give up, but every time there was an impasse, they returned with a new set of options and structures.

I'm so pleased to acknowledge that the succession planning was completely successful both for our business and each stakeholder personally. I believe the business and family is stronger because of the process. We are ready to move on to the next generation! It's easy for me to recommend reading *Buying Out the Boss* because I was part of not only buying out one boss but three of them! Enjoy reading and enjoy working with Kevin and Mike.

TODD MARION, PRESIDENT AND CEO
MARION EXCAVATING CO. INC.

INTRODUCTION

By all appearances, the Howard family is what people think of when they think of a successful business. The family construction business is now into its fourth generation. The first generation started the business in the 1920s. It was transitioned to their three children, who kept the business prosperous until the early 1990s. Then, like many typical family businesses, a number of children from the third generation worked in the business and went on to employ some of their children—the fourth generation. The business by now had two different operating divisions, one operated by one family and the other by the second. The third family wasn't active in the business at all.

When the time came for the second generation to do their succession planning, they decided it was in the families' collective best interest to keep both divisions together and operating as one company. The third generation didn't get along with one another all that well, however, and both sides were far more interested in what was best for their division, not the overall company. The third family still had an equal stake in the company, even though they were inactive. They were only interested in what they could take out of the business. The equal ownership and control limited what they could do in terms of growing the business, passing it on to the next generation, or cashing out from it.

Because of the governance structure, as time went by, one of the three third-generation Howards was always a pivot point to get whatever they wanted out of the mix with the other ones. They were also competitive with one another, so they put their individual operation ahead of the overall company. Over time, they failed to make investments in the business, and it began to decline.

Finally, one family member just wanted to get out. The mechanism the second generation had put in place to do that was perceived as being grossly unfair—it handcuffed the next generations so that they could never receive their value. That family member was only interested in getting money out, but the terms made it very unattractive. That only further prolonged the mess.

Our firm was engaged to try to find a way to break them up fairly. Initially, we wondered, "How can you fix this?"

The smartest thing to do was to separate the companies, but by this point, the families had reached a point of such deep-seated dislike that we couldn't get them to come to an agreement. We were at the one-yard line more than once, and then one of the parties would change their minds or would get greedier.

After a lot of fruitless negotiation, the business is now shut down. The families have lost hundreds of thousands of dollars. In all likelihood, no one will get anything out of the whole transaction. This fourth-generation business will not make it to the fifth generation. The plan of the second generation was to create a lasting structure that would pass the business on and provide for everybody. It did the opposite. It's tragic to see a very successful business, one worth perhaps five million dollars, go into receivership instead. How different would the business and family be today if instead of allowing the second generation to decide their future, the third generation had made the decision to buy out the boss?

DEATH OF A BUSINESS

The root of the Howard family problem was twofold: poor planning and the expectation that there would always be harmony in the business. There was never a recognition that the shareholders within the family might come to have different interests.

The real failure for the Howards was the assumption that all future generations would get along and that their interests would continue to be aligned. That was fine when the business was doing well, when there were only three shareholders, and when everyone involved was capable of and interested in running the company. There was no functional mechanism for dealing with fundamental disagreements, personality clashes, and lack of ability among the later generation of cousins. At one point there were fifteen different shareholders, although most of them weren't active in the business. Even so, because of the governance structure, they had as much say as those who were active. The problems only got worse as the business declined. At the end of the day, the shareholders weren't flexible. All they wanted to know was, "How much money can I take out of this?" and "How miserable can I make everyone else?"

The older generation of Howards thought that by treating everyone equally, they were doing the right thing to preserve the business. Everyone goes into succession planning with the philosophy that they're doing what's right. In this case, they never explored the possibility that passing the business on this way might not take personalities and capabilities into consideration. They never chose or groomed a successor to run it as one company, either because they felt no one was capable or because they didn't want to create more conflict. This happens often with businesses; the desire to treat everyone equally when they aren't overrides common sense. Successful succession plans frequently require very hard conversations and decisions. The second generation of Howards were unwilling to do that work. More importantly, no one from the third generation stepped up to challenge the families' conventional wisdom. A successor needs to be prepared to take control.

A DIFFERENT APPROACH

By contrast, we also represent a business that has a founding patriarch and matriarch, four children in the business, and thirteen grandchildren. The kids and grandkids were all brought up to respect one another and work together in the business. Because the patriarch is a dynastic thinker who looks to the long term, the governance he has put in place will make it possible for the business to continue into the next generations with a more realistic corporate structure. Any grandchild who's interested can come into the business, but there's a mechanism for getting them in—and also a mechanism for those who don't want to join. Just as important is the fact that this family has a much better ability to communicate well with one another. The transition to the third generation won't be seamless and without conflict, but it will still be a good transition, because all the planning and governance models are in place.

THE EVOLUTION OF SUCCESSION PLANNING

We see businesses like the Howards' all too often. They work with attorneys and accountants to put agreements together, but they don't think through the impacts. They don't think about how succession is going to affect each party and what everyone needs and wants. They think of the ownership of the business as a privilege—which it is—but fail to fully recognize the burdens that come with it for the successor. That's where we come in. The Vann Group can look beyond the paperwork to see the perspective of the buyer, not just the perspective of a founder looking to exit. That buyer might be one or more family members, or often the buyer is an insider—a key employee or perhaps several employees.

For more than thirty-five years, our firm has been helping sellers and buyers come together. No two cases are ever the same, so we can take a lot of lessons from them. We see it all. For example, there's Mr. Lewis. He's well into his eighties and owns more than thirty different rental properties. He's very successful, except when it comes to succession planning. He hasn't done any of that at all. The situation is complicated, because some of his kids work in the business and some don't. He has a second wife with some financial interest in the business, and there's an ex-wife with a trust who also has a financial interest.

The children are themselves in their sixties and contemplating their own retirement. The problem is a total lack of planning for succession. No operating agreements are in place—no structure whatsoever—because Mr. Lewis is convinced he's going to live forever. At the same time, when we say, "This is what you need to do," his children respond, "Boy, that's going to cost us a lot of money that we'd rather not spend." They don't recognize that they're going to spend a lot more than that when their father passes and the battle over the succession begins.

The selfishness and lack of vision in these situations usually comes from either the family matriarch or the patriarch. The dysfunction comes from the heirs. One day, Mr. Lewis is going to be gone, and then—because he wouldn't deal with the succession—lawyers, accountants, the IRS, and the state are going to deal with it instead. Some of the kids are in the business and want it to continue, but the others will want to cash out. There's no mechanism in place for that to happen.

THE VANN GROUP

We have an entrepreneurial family, going all the way back to the early 1800s. Our passion is for business; we own several today. When you grow up with a business background and go into consulting and transactions, you learn to solve a lot of problems and do crisis planning—and you learn to deal with conflict, privilege, and bias when creating the plans for the transfer of a business. We appreciate the intricacies of succession planning because we also own a company that had intergenerational family issues. The business was started by two uncles who, at this point, haven't spoken to each other in years. Seven cousins in the family had minority interests in this good-sized company. Five of them have left the business, leaving two to run it. Because of the family dysfunction, planning for the future is very difficult.

We've been consulting for clients for more than thirty-five years, dealing with those same issues of succession, whether within the family, or as a nonfamily transfer. The Vann Group today brings our knowledge and experience to business transfers. Our goal with this book is to help business buyers and business owners understand the complexities of transferring a business successfully from the current owners to their successors, whether those successors are family members, insider employees, or outsiders. Our advice is based on our practical experience with hundreds of clients over the years.

We want to help keep the business in the family, if that's what they want. If not, we want to help employees or an outside buyer make the best deal possible to keep the company going. We want to help them buy out the boss. Plus, we like the challenge of putting together a good deal.

Succession planning can be so complicated that, ideally, you would begin it from day one, when you start the business. Realistically, there's a five-year window from the time you start to think that maybe it's time to retire and pass the business on, to the time it actually happens. Before that, there should always be some planning done to protect your family and the business in the event the worst case happens. Most business owners leave succession planning for much later in the game, but it's never too late to get started.

There's a real need for succession planning today. Demographics tell us that the biggest transition of business ownership ever is coming up, but most of the businesses involved, which are a significant portion of individual wealth, aren't positioned to be sold. In this book, we hope to provide the dose of reality that buyers need. We want to help them understand the nuances and dynamics of what goes on in the emotional side of a business and how to apply that understanding to the purchase process. Sometimes we feel like family therapists, rather than business consultants, but our job is to be the business's best friend and arrange the best deal for everyone.

WHY THIS BOOK AND THIS TOPIC

As a father-and-son team, we've always wanted to write a book but could never find the time or the right topic. Then, one day it hit us. There is so much activity in the succession and transition planning space, but it is all focused on the seller. If you go to Amazon or Google, the succession planning section, you'll find countless books, websites, and firms dedicated to the topic.

When we started looking at it objectively, we found that everyone has advice and guidance for the seller on how to do a plan and execute a transaction, but we couldn't find a resource that looked at the transition from the perspective of the buyer. The buyer is inherently disadvantaged when the process begins. They have less business experience and generally don't have the team of long-term advisors to guide them and the resources to get them.

When we looked back at our most successful internal transitions, we found that all had had an educated buyer. The buyers who became these successors were either smart enough or lucky enough to figure it out. If the adage "Knowing is half the battle" is true, then a successful transition has to have a knowledgeable buyer as well as seller.

We've written this book to provide buyers with the knowledge they need to start the process. We also hope that our sellers will read the book so they understand the buyer's perspective. An internal transition is a wonderful result, but it can't happen without that knowledge.

WHAT YOU'LL LEARN

We've broken this book into three parts: Prepare, Advance, and Close. In part I, Prepare, we'll explore the basics of succession planning in chapter 1. In chapter 2, we'll go on to discuss the four key elements of every transaction. Then in chapter 3, we'll talk about opening Pandora's box—all the unpleasant issues that can arise when the succession issue is brought up. Chapter 4 will explain how buyers can put together a good working team of advisors.

Part II, Advance, explores ways to move the deal forward. In chapter 5, we'll clarify the process and discuss the basics of expectations, valuation, and realities. Chapter 6 will go more deeply into ways to set expectations for the deal that both parties can agree to. Assessing the value of the company will be explained in chapter 7, and chapter 8 will deal with reconciling the realities: how to bridge the gap between what the seller needs and what the buyer wants. The strategy needed to reach an agreement is the subject of chapter 9. In chapter 10, we get down to the mechanics of the deal, including due diligence, payment structure, and tax and legal issues.

Part III, Close, clarifies the steps to closing the deal. Chapter 11 talks about the many ways the deal could be financed. Chapter 12 explores all the ways the deal could fall apart at the last minute, ways to avoid that outcome, and how to keep the deal moving forward. In chapter 13, we talk about transition planning for the new owner and strategies for avoiding the common business culture problems that come with change. We point out an often overlooked issue—legacy costs—for new owners in chapter 14. And finally, in chapter 15, we explain how value building helps ensure future success.

Succession planning isn't easy. There's a lot to know, a lot that can't be fully anticipated, and a lot that can go wrong. But with the knowledge you'll gain from this book, you'll learn how to make things go right and negotiate a successful transfer.

If you're giving some thought to buying out the boss, it's time to get started. We'll begin with the basics of an inside deal.

PART I

PREPARE

1

THE BASICS

KD Dynamics Tool Company, a precision manufacturer of engine components, took us on a wild ride through the transition process and back again. The company was started by a very successful entrepreneur who had a number of business interests that were occupying his time and energy. A key employee wanted to buy the business. The entrepreneur wanted to sell, the employee wanted to buy, so they made a quick deal. The problem was, it was a top-of-the-market deal that was highly leveraged. The buyer was in way over his head, but he'd been running the business and thought he could manage the payments. He was confident, the banks were confident, and the deal went through. Six months later, the recession hit, the business tanked, and the bank foreclosed.

What went wrong? The inside buyer was too confident. He placed too much emphasis on his knowledge of the opportunity rather than exploring the risks. He didn't look at the risk factors and didn't take into consideration the reality that he was undercapitalized. He anticipated growth, which would allow him to pay off the purchase, but he left himself with no room for error and no room for the unanticipated. Because of the recession, the business declined and couldn't survive with the debt load.

The original owner was able to buy the business back from the bank for pennies on the dollar. Today, he once again owns the business—and the buyer is back to working for him. The company is doing very, very well. The big loser was the bank, of course, but also the buyer. He had put up his house as collateral and had also borrowed heavily from family. When he went into personal bankruptcy, he had some severe financial and family pressures as a result of the deal.

INSIDER VERSUS OUTSIDER

An insider buying out the boss is in a different position than an outside buyer. As an insider, whether you're a longtime employee or a family member, you know the business. You know things that someone on the outside doesn't. That creates both a tremendous advantage and an unexpected disadvantage when you're thinking of buying the business. On the plus side, you know things no outsider can know. You know where the bodies are buried; you know the personality traits and the quirks of the owners and other employees, and how to push their buttons. The disadvantage is you know these things. Sometimes that can cloud your judgment.

Your relationship with the owner might be good, it might be bad, or it might be love-hate. Whatever it's like, your personal biases can put blinders on you when it comes to handling the sale. You may think you know the seller well, but you've never dealt with them in this situation. Quite frequently, buyers are surprised when it comes to talking money with the seller. As soon as the discussions start, the dynamics in the relationship change. The seller's objectives ultimately are to maximize the price and protect their interest. Likewise, the buyer's objectives are to minimize the price and protect their interest. No matter how close you were with the boss, you now have competing interests. That puts a lot of pressure on the working relationship.

There's more at risk with an inside sale. If somebody from outside, whom the seller doesn't know, tries to make a deal and it falls through—well, it falls through, and there are no hard feelings. But if an employee or a family member tries to make a deal and it falls through, that individual is still working for the seller. What happens to their relationship and their job, then?

We worked with a business in which the kids were negotiating to buy from their parents. We put a fair market value on it, but the father said, "This isn't enough money. You want me pushing carts at the grocery store when I'm seventy-four years old?" The kids were under pressure to come up with more money so that their parents would be taken care of in their retirement. On the other hand, Dad shouldn't have expected to get a premium on the business just because he hadn't done any planning. The situation caused a lot of family conflict, both at work and at home. We were able to structure the deal in a way that gave him somewhat more money, but there are limitations, even when the family buys the business.

If you're an insider, you've got a good perspective on where the flaws in the business are and where the traps might be. But as an insider, it's sometimes very difficult to ask the tough questions required by due diligence. You may not want to ask a question that's going to affect your relationship with the boss, another employee, or another department or division. As an insider, you think, "I'll worry about that later." You tend to overlook the flaws. An outsider, however, thinks, "I don't know much about this business. I'm going to spend a lot of time and money digging as deep as I possibly can and I'm going to ask those hard questions."

A good example is the payroll. As an insider, you might be aware that the boss's wife is on the payroll for a hundred grand a year but doesn't do anything to earn it. You'd be reluctant to question that when you go through the books. In fact, that's such a sensitive issue that the boss might not even want to show you the payroll. But an outside buyer would have no problem asking that question and insisting on seeing the relevant documents. The insider's advantage, however, is they know who's overpaid, who performs, who produces, and who doesn't.

THE TWELVE LAWS OF THE DEAL

Over the years, we've developed twelve laws that apply to every insider deal. If you bear them in mind, your chances of being successful in buying out the boss will improve.

ALL BUSINESS IS PERSONAL.

That line comes from the novel *The Godfather*. In the movie, the line was changed to "It's not personal, Michael; it's just business." The book got it right. You put everything on the line when you own a business. You put your family, your way of life, your ego, your wealth, and your time on the line. All business is personal. It's personal to you and it's most definitely personal to the seller. Always demonstrate a healthy respect for the personal nature of the business when putting a deal together.

BE SMART—KNOW EVERYTHING YOU CAN.

You've got to listen and learn and understand the nuances while you do the deal. Don't just rely on your attorney or accountant to say, "This is good," or "This is bad." Don't be too trusting. Have the knowledge yourself. If you don't know something, find out.

Don't be afraid to question your advisors. Because of the lingo in the industry, they may be talking over your head—we do it sometimes, even though we try not to. There are no dumb questions—make sure you listen carefully to the answers. When you're excited about buying the business, you may not have the perspective to see it the way it is at the moment, rather than as you hope it will become.

CHOOSE GOOD ADVISORS WHO KNOW HOW TO CLOSE DEALS.

Good advisors are critical to your success. You need lawyers, accountants, financial planners, and business consultants like us. You also need trusted mentors—anyone who has the experience to tell you what it takes to close the deal successfully and help you stay calm and objective.

Experience is key. Just because someone is an attorney doesn't mean she can draft and go through commercial transactions effectively. You may not want the lawyer who handled your divorce handling your purchase. If you're searching for referrals to the best people, try talking to your local commercial bankers. They know who's good and who isn't, and will refer you to capable advisors. (We'll talk more about how to build a great team in chapter 4.)

WHAT'S GOOD FOR THE BUYER ISN'T GOOD FOR THE SELLER.

You need to find a balance between what's good for the buyer and what's good for the seller. You have to be willing to give a little bit and come to a compromise instead of an impasse. Also remember, the more of the deal the seller is financing, the more likely it is that you will be compromising a bit more than you would like.

THE BUYER PROBABLY DOESN'T HAVE ENOUGH MONEY TO DO THE DEAL.

As a buyer, you almost certainly don't have enough cash on hand to do the deal. You're going to have to borrow, most likely from both the bank and the seller. You'll also probably have to fill in a gap and borrow from the three Fs: friends, families, and fools. (We'll discuss ways to finance your deal in more detail in chapter 11.)

SELLER FINANCING (FOR MORE THAN THEY WANT) IS NECESSARY.

If you're the average entrepreneurial buyer, you're in your mid-forties, you own a home and have a family, and you don't have a lot of liquid wealth. Seller financing is going to be necessary—and it's going to have to be for more than the seller wants. Everyone wants to get all or mostly cash when they sell their business, but that doesn't usually happen. You're also probably going to have to finance more than you want. (We'll go into ways to finance the deal in detail in chapter 11.)

DEAL KILLERS WILL ARISE AT THE MOST INCONVENIENT TIME.

There's never a good time for a deal-killing issue to arise, but they always seem to come up at the most inconvenient time—including at the closing and even afterward. Sometimes the deal killer is emotional: greed or ego. Sometimes it's something that was uncovered at the last minute by due diligence. We had one case in which due diligence uncovered an environmental health issue with the building being sold, just as the deal was about to close. It didn't kill the deal, but it caused a lot of problems and cost a lot of money. More commonly, last-minute issues over money or employment can derail the deal. For example, a key employee may decide not to stay on because the company is changing hands—that can kill the deal. (For more on deal killers and how to get past them, see chapter 12.)

IT'S NOT THE SALE PRICE; IT'S THE NET.

The actual selling price of the company matters far less than what the seller nets at the closing. The sale price is like your paycheck. You don't care what the gross is before deductions. You want to know what you're taking home.

We did one deal where the sellers had a strong inside offer. It was a stock deal, all in cash. That meant the sellers were going to pay the lowest possible tax rate on the gain, and that there would be no risk to them regarding earnouts or seller financing. Even though they were going to get more money than they'd originally projected, they still weren't happy with it, because the total number wasn't high enough. They should have focused on the net price.

THE NUMBERS DON'T LIE.

You can only do so much with the numbers when it comes to financing, whether with a bank or anyone else. The seller may show you the tax returns and the financials but also tell you that they're not the full story. What they're reporting to the government isn't the real income, because they were taking cash out in some way. Illegality and ethics aside, when you go to a lender to borrow, they will look only at the documents, and the documents may not justify the amount you want to borrow.

When the numbers are real and honest, the seller may still want more money than the value of the company can support. One of our clients was convinced that he should put a much higher value on the company than it was really worth. He was sure he could get the full asking price because anyone who took over could come in and make more money than he did. But the current value is what counts—the cash flow would only support financing at a lower price. Wishful thinking doesn't work.

BANKS AREN'T INVESTORS AND THEY DON'T LIKE RISK.

Conventional lenders don't see themselves as investors. All the bank wants is to be paid back with interest. They're very conservative when it comes to risk—they take a rigid approach to lending, because the regulators and the credit department strictly limit what they can do. A banker once told us, "We're allowed a delinquency rate of one-and-a-half, maybe two, percent of our total asset base." That means they have to be right more than 98 percent of the time on their loans, otherwise they're out of business. That doesn't give them much capacity to take a risk.

If you have a good deal that makes sense, and you've got

some down payment money, and the seller's going to do some financing, and the company has a good financial history, go to the bank. More likely than not, you'll get a good deal with good terms.

If some of those pieces aren't in place, as a buyer you need to find a lender that has more flexibility but will charge you a bit more. You'll have to go with an unconventional lender. These go by a lot of names: nonconforming lending, gap lenders, mezzanine lenders, angel investors, peer-to-peer lenders. You can go online today and probably raise $150,000, but you're going to pay a premium for that.

THERE'S NO SUCH THING AS A WIN-WIN DEAL.

All our clients start out telling us, "We just want a win-win deal." Well, that never happens. A good deal is when both sides end up a little disappointed. Not so disappointed that they're later sorry they did the deal, or so disappointed they back out, but just disappointed enough to realize they can't get everything that they want as a buyer or a seller. After all, when you don't get the steak cooked exactly the way you want it, you can still eat it.

YOU ARE RESPONSIBLE FOR THE SINS OF THE OWNER.

When you buy the company, you'll discover things you

didn't necessarily know about and that weren't uncovered during due diligence. Or maybe you knew about them and went ahead anyway. You still have to deal with them. For example, you might find customers who have special considerations for their terms and conditions, or an employee who's overpaid because the previous owners didn't want to lose her, or maybe the company is stuck with a bad lease.

To take one example, we have a client who never had uniform terms and conditions for their sales. It's always been very informal, but the new owner wants to get things on a more consistent footing. He's discovering that it's difficult to do that with the company's long-standing customers.

You may also have to deal with a situation in which the previous owner didn't want to deal with an issue, such as a problem employee; now it's up to you to fix it instead. (See chapter 13 for ideas on how to develop your transition plan.)

In our experience, every one of the twelve rules influences every step in the deal-making process. Keep that in mind as we break apart and explain the elements of a deal in the next chapter.

2

THE ELEMENTS

One of our clients, Alice, who's been with us for many years—she's a dear friend, actually—owns an architectural firm. Alice is in her late seventies and recently approached us to help her value the business and find a buyer.

We valued the business, headed out into the market, and found a couple of buyers. However, we ran into a problem: Alice's comfort level was low, because she had no confidence any of these buyers would keep her team in place. Alice had worked incredibly hard over the years to build a high-end and profitable firm with great service, great quality, and great employee culture. She paid her team well; for example, she paid the business's manager much higher than scale. She felt that a better solution than an outside buyout would be to put together a plan for her four key managers to buy the business.

These four key managers had very different roles. One was a practicing architect, one was in business development, one was working in a CFO capacity, and one was a project manager. Alice felt that there were no other people out there that better fit those roles than her own existing team, and she wanted that team to continue to thrive.

We helped her put together a plan by which these four managers could come together as business partners. Alice would offer them the business at a huge discount—30 or 40 percent—and she'd finance it for them, because she knew they wouldn't have much luck securing financing from a bank. The plan was that her estate would hold the loan, and she and her daughter would stay on as trustees of the business. The way she saw it, she could maintain the amazing culture she'd built. She and her former employees, now owners, could all be one big happy family while running the business.

When we were ready to present the plan to the new potential owners, we met them for dinner one night at their office. We rolled out our entire plan, soup to nuts, with a ton of confidence and excitement. We showed them how they could get in on a profitable business with almost no risk, while keeping their team and culture intact. We left that dinner feeling sky-high, thinking, "I wish I were one of those four!" The opportunity was just that fantastic, and it was simply being handed to them.

Days went by. Soon, it became clear that all the excitement that had been brewing around the deal and the idea itself was weighted toward the seller side—us and Alice. The potential new ownership team? They weren't as excited. We couldn't understand it at first, but then we started to see what was happening. Even though the four employees had operated as a successful management team, when they'd considered entering into the deeper relationship of business ownership, the façade of a happy team had crumbled. They'd started picking out all the negatives in one another's personalities. They'd come up with every reason in the book why they wouldn't want to go into business together. There was constant nitpicking. Baggage had appeared out of nowhere, like we'd crashed a plane and the baggage had tumbled out!

As the situation grew more and more emotional, the potential buyers lost sight of the incredible opportunity in front of them. Instead, they circled around one another, planting flags and switching camps—and the worst part was, they didn't stay quiet. They let their feelings about one another resonate through the entire firm; they ranted to their spouses at home. The deal became a total cluster of emotions.

Much to Alice's dismay, and ours, it all fell apart. The emotion, not the strategy we'd laid out, blew that deal away. The risk we'd taken was substantial. A high-functioning strategic management team, which has previously been held together with the strongest fiber, was now in pieces. All the accusations and office politics created huge risk within the organization. Alice saw this, and the appeal of selling to her management team fell away. She became disenchanted with the whole idea.

Since that time, Alice's relationship with her four key employees has been completely different. She's still close with them, but it isn't the way it used to be. The architect on the management team had been incredibly disappointed that the offer had become such a personal battle. He had some serious potential as a businessperson and was still interested in purchasing the business. Unfortunately, he couldn't afford to do it himself. He had, however, been a key player in a division of the business in another state. We were able to spin out that division and recapitalize it. He and Alice are now partners in that business, and he signed a long-term agreement not only to operate it on her behalf but also to purchase the balance of the business through the estate.

That part was a success, but it was only one-fourth of a success that should have been 100 percent. Emotion simply tore apart a great plan. We'd thought that plan was a true gift to valued employees. To have it fall apart like that was like someone opening a gift you gave them and saying, "I hate this. Send it back!" It hurt us, it hurt them, they hurt one another, and in the end, the emotional tension wasn't sustainable. That management team has never been the same.

The potential pressure of guaranteeing debt by buying the business disrupted the balance of egos among the employees. Alice had kept those egos in check while she ran the company, but with her gone, they were unleashed, and not in a good way. Fortunately, Alice regrouped, and we are pleased to report that Alice, her daughter, and the Vann Group have formed a new management team. Two of the managers are presently entering into agreements to become owners.

As Alice's story demonstrates, the emotional component of a transaction can never be underestimated. No matter how good a strategic plan looks on paper, no matter how generous the offer is, feelings drive the destiny of the deal. At gut check time, Alice's team wasn't comfortable. With all our experience, we could see that this was a great deal for the buyers. Because we assumed we'd go through with it in a heartbeat, we assumed they would, too. But the egos, the jealousies, the history—it all came together in a way we didn't anticipate. It was a perfect plan with an anything-but-perfect ending.

ASSUMPTIONS AND REALITY

Another side to the downfall was Alice's assumptions. She thought that as the owner, she had the power to decide the way it was going to be: "I'm going to sell to my team; they're great. This is how I want it to be." But she hadn't done the work of having the conversations and understanding the nuances before making that assumption. She thought she knew her people better than she really did.

Assumptions about relationships can screw up a transaction. You might expect all your employees or family members to be on the same page regarding a certain issue. At the end of the day, though, you might discover they don't agree at all, all because you forgot to ask them. With Alice's team, we didn't have that exploratory conversation. We came in to make the presentation, dressed in a suit and tie, and laid it out over a big dinner. There was never any earlier dialogue asking if they were even interested. We just took for granted that they were. That's a dangerous assumption and a mistake we've learned not to make again.

Owners and entrepreneurs sometimes find it hard to understand that not everyone wants to be in their shoes. We look at things from the context of "This is a great opportunity for you to own something, to have your shot." Any owner can only see the positive aspects of the opportunity, but there are reasons people choose to be employed.

Owners think that their succession plan is going to reward key employees who've been dedicated and loyal by giving them the business. They often have a lack of awareness as to what those employees truly want and what drives them.

In Alice's case, she had given her team several indications that something was in the works. They'd all been concerned about her age and were wondering what would happen upon her retirement. She had reassured them on several occasions, telling them she was at work on a plan that "is going to be great for everybody." Ultimately, in their view, it was great for only one person.

Owners should keep in mind, too, that today employees tend to be more concerned about their quality of life than in the past. Alice's employees knew, because they had watched for years, how hard Alice worked. They were going to have to work that hard if they took over the company. The quality of life equation entered strongly into their thinking.

If we had pitched Alice's offer to the four team members twenty years ago, we're sure they would have bought in blindfolded. After our initial presentation, however, there was lots of discussion about quality of life: Am I going to have to work more hours? Will my husband or wife support it? Can I still pick up my kids after school every day? We would never have heard that twenty years ago.

We thought, "It's a gift." They said they didn't want the gift; they didn't like the color. Things have changed.

As owners, we tend to take for granted that others want the stress of being self-employed. But families, especially spouses, and certainly other employees, look at the owner and think, "They're a workaholic, they're always stressed out. Why would I want that?"

We're owners and business advisors, so we think, "Why would you not want this opportunity? Pick yourself up. Go for it!" We think of this grind as a natural way of life; most people, however, think we've got a screw loose.

THE KEY ELEMENTS OF EVERY TRANSACTION

EMOTION

A deal lets you experience all the highs and lows of life in the space of thirty seconds. Everything's new; if you're the buyer or seller, it's likely the first time you've done this. Unless you're a true serial entrepreneur, this is probably the most important transaction you'll ever effect. Sellers have often built their whole lives around their business. Their identity is wrapped around it. The business has provided a lifestyle for their family, security for their kids, and it's given them their social identity. It's all very, very personal to them. When it comes time to sell, they go through an incredible range of emotions because it's not "just a business." It's their baby; it's their mistress. Letting go brings up all kinds of feelings. It's as though they're obsessed.

For buyers, things are a bit different. There's a fear factor to it. They're potentially taking on a tremendous amount of risk. The buyer may or may not have any emotional attachment to the business; they may operate from a more clinical perspective. Sellers generally see opportunity with business. Buyers are more likely to see risk.

When you get into a transaction, the devil is in the details, and those details can be incredibly frustrating. They swing your mood one way and then another on any given day. We can't tell you how many deals have died at two o'clock and have been brought back to life by 2:30. They're triggered by emotions: "I'm not giving him another ten grand, I don't care!" "No, I'm not giving in on this little point!"

As a buyer, you've got to manage not only your own emotional volatility, but you've got to manage the emotions of everyone else involved in the transaction. Your advisors have been through this before, but your spouse, family, and friends are just as emotional as you. Your spouse or partner, especially, has a vested interest in what happens in this transaction.

If you're going to have success in buying a company, you

need to understand the emotions, mindset, and drives of the people involved. For instance, if an owner is very invested in his legacy, he might take less money if he feels assured his legacy will endure. Emotion can be a huge factor for key employees and family members. The tension can even be worse for employees, who fear being marginalized by family members; they might fear the "blood is thicker than water" mindset.

Who's the Boss You Want to Buy?

The deal is very different if you're buying from Mom and Dad versus Dad and Stepmom, or if you're buying from your boss. You've got to keep in mind whom you're acquiring and what that relationship is, and what could be the potential fallout. If you're buying the family business, are you getting the opportunity to buy it but your sister isn't? What happens from there? It's not uncommon when parents sell a business that there's even a disagreement between the two of them on what they should be doing for each child in a transaction.

You might think that when it comes to passing on a family business, the transaction would be friendly, but often it's not. We worked with a distributor where the son had to pay fair market value for the company, because Dad needed the money. On top of that, Dad kept the son—who'd bought the company at full price—out of his will, rationalizing that he'd already given his son this great opportunity. While he couldn't have bought the company if it wasn't his father who owned it, on some levels it was probably worse for him because he was buying from his dad. He was penalized for taking over the business and contributing to his father's financial security. In this case, legacy costs cost a lot. To this day, we're still advising on this transaction, because other legacy costs have popped up.

The lesson here? It's critical to consider how your relationships are going to be impacted if you're buying out a family member.

Through the Looking Glass

Once you sit down to do the transaction, everything changes for both parties—you're never going to look at that person the same way again. If things come together, things will change. If the transaction fails, things will change.

People think all sorts of negative things, "I thought I knew you well, but now you're going to screw me...I thought I knew you better, that you'd make me a better offer...You were brutal to negotiate with...I never realized you didn't like my wife."

We once had a client where the father and son never had

a great relationship. The father was very tough on his kids, ragging on them constantly when they were growing up. Despite that, the son still went into the family insurance business. He worked hard and he got small raises. We put together a purchase plan for him and he's now buying his father out, 10 percent every year. He's discovered that the more he buys out, the worse their relationship gets. They dislike each other so much now that they don't do anything together; family events are awkward. He can't wait until his father is out of the picture. Sadly, the relationship has deteriorated so much that even this process has stopped.

Family dynamics can change once we get an agreement. We've even had parents try to back out of agreements made with their own kids. It's not unusual for a parent to come in and say, "You know, I think I made a mistake. I don't think we got the best deal. You were leaning a little bit more toward the next generation." We can't go back and change a legal document unless there are provisions for a buyback. You can't just lend the company to the kids.

Barry is an example of a parent who couldn't let go after he sold the business to his daughter, Lisa. The relationship with both her parents has changed. Lisa had been a high-performing employee for a decade. She bought the business under her father's terms and conditions. He's not questioning whether he sold it to her too cheap; rather, he can't let go. She wants to run the business without disruption, but Barry has a tendency to stop by unexpectedly and linger in the plant, offering his two cents, interfering in the day-to-day business, and compromising her authority. She's a grown woman and wants to be treated like the president, CEO, and owner of the business, but he still wants to treat her like daddy's little girl.

In Lisa's case, the family strains have been worth it. She's succeeded and built the business to be a very successful enterprise. She carries herself well; she's respected and has created a great life for her husband and children. She goes home tired and sometimes frustrated at the end of the day, but she's enjoying operating the business. That's worth a lot, if it's your passion.

Your Appetite for Risk

Whenever you want to buy out the boss, there's a risk that things won't work out. As a buyer, the biggest hurdle is being comfortable with the debt you're taking on. Most buyers will need to put all their cash into the transaction and then guarantee notes to the bank or seller. Those notes are likely to be more than your net worth. One of our clients had a conversation with his wife, who asked how much they'd be borrowing for an upcoming purchase. When he said several million, she said, "We don't have that." He replied, "Yeah. We don't need to worry because it's more money than we can ever pay back!" It will keep you up at night, borrowing millions, or at least an amount that's far more than you can imagine paying back.

Besides the money, you must understand that you'll be taking risks with all your relationships in and around the business. Everything changes when you become the boss. Coworkers are no longer coworkers. You have a different relationship with your clients. These new relationships can be rewarding, but there will be a learning curve.

We've found that many of our younger clients are more risk-averse than older generations. They're cautious with the decisions they make and don't have the "we don't care how much we owe; we're going to win" approach that prior generations did. Their mindset is geared toward short-term investment and risk, which doesn't fit well with buying a business. Many are burdened by school debt and memories of growing up in the Great Recession.

They also see their parents living on the edge financially, overextended and unable to save. Mom and Dad are in their late fifties and sixties and are still cosigning student loans while also having car loans, mortgages, and home equity loans. Their parents are still working because they weren't able to save. The kids see that and say, "I don't want to live like my parents. I don't want that risk. I don't want that debt."

Gut Check Time

When it's time to pull the trigger, you've got to be all in—and so does your spouse or partner. We've seen many deals collapse because the significant other was uncomfortable with the debt they were being asked to secure or weren't on board with the lifestyle change. With your spouse or partner, you have to make sure they've thrown out the rose-colored glasses and are in touch with reality; we work hard to make sure the spouses or whoever's at the table understands everything that's going on.

We had a recent sale of a retailer and the wife was nervous about the debt. She worried that they'd never be able to pay back the debt if it didn't work out. We pointed out, "No, you won't be able to pay it if you come home every night and worry about it." That mentality is ruinous. Family support is extremely important when you're going off on your own.

THE QUESTIONS TO ASK
Can You Get the Boss to Do a Deal?

We've had sellers who'll talk all day long about selling their business but won't pull the trigger. You have to ask yourself, "Is he really a seller?"

We consider several things to determine this. First, how do they engage with the business? Are they obsessed with it? Do they come in at 6:00 a.m. and stay until 8:00 p.m.? That owner may not be able to let go. On the other hand, you might have the owner who's checked out. They come in but only go through the motions.

Do you know what the owner's financial situation is? We often assume owners are rich, but by looking at their spending habits, you may see they may not have the ability to make a deal.

In the case of the distributor we discussed earlier, the price for the business was full market value—no family discount. It was that price because it had to be. The father had an extremely expensive lifestyle—alimony, several kids, condos and vacation homes, vehicles, travel, and entertainment. He wasn't going to sell at a discount because he couldn't afford to. We were able to be creative and structure something that worked for the son, but only because we were able to leverage our inside knowledge of the situation to help the buy side. We cut a good side deal for Dad, but money is still an issue.

Can You Live with the Lifestyle?

For buyers, the quality-of-life change after the purchase can be dramatic. You don't get to go home at 5:00 p.m. anymore. If there's a problem, you're the one who's dealing with it. And when you do go home, when you get up in the middle of the night to go to the bathroom, it's still on your mind. We always tell spouses and family when they come in that once you buy a business, there's a part of you that's always driven by it. You were driven to buy this business, and then once you pull the trigger, you become driven by the need to be successful with it.

You're likely to become more driven by the success of your business than you are by the success of your home life. We say this and people balk. They say, sometimes very heatedly, "That will never happen!" But you change when you become a business owner. Your earlier measures of success–how many of your kids' ball games you attended, how much time you spent with your spouse— might change.

Your new scorecard in life could be landing a great contract or a new account—not attending a family event. The balance of your life changes, but it's not as though you're loving your work more than your family. We suggest you sit down with your family and explain to your kids and spouse how things might change. You might say, "Mom or Dad won't be able to come to your game at 4:30 in the afternoon," or "I won't be home for dinner every night," but that doesn't mean there's less love. If your vocation is to build birdhouses in your basement and you don't go upstairs for dinner every night because you're building birdhouses, well, that's your passion and it's the shape of your life. It's not because you don't love your family or are having an affair. It's the same as if you have a passion for tennis and don't come home for dinner on Sundays. The truth is, a lot of people work long hours and obsess about work who don't own the business. If that's your nature, you might as well own it!

Can You Accept the Stress?

Like many of the lifestyle issues and risks of becoming an owner, it's your attitude and mindset that are going to dictate your success. If you and your family see becoming an owner as a hardship, that's going to become a problem. Ask to what degree your family is going to support you in this. What level of stress are you prepared to handle? Buyers always underestimate how stressful owning will be—otherwise, they wouldn't buy. Employee-buyers, though, often know what they're getting into. A silver lining for them is it might be less stressful to own the business than run it!

Over the last twenty years, the pace of daily life has accelerated and that can mean, as an owner, you're cycling through many more emotions and decisions over the course of the day. It used to be you'd have a bad day in the week or a bad day in the month, and the business would suffer for a short time. Today, because everything moves so fast, you can have multiple ups and downs over the course of a day. You can have a great Monday morning and then be ready to jump out the window on Monday afternoon.

If your personality lends itself to flexibility and letting go of what you can't control, you'll do better. We have the wisdom of experience that makes things much easier than earlier in our careers, but even so, we'd say the stress on business owners is a hundred times what it used to be. Employees are under more stress, too, so sometimes you have to deal with unhappy employees. Their stress becomes your stress.

What Separates a Good Decision from a Bad Decision?

There's an old expression, "Making no decision can be worse than making a bad one." There's a lot truth to that, especially as a leader. Sometimes the overanalyzing can be a form of procrastination and the extra data doesn't help. But in general, even making a bad decision means you're moving forward and that momentum can lead to good decisions. The more knowledge a buyer has, the less you'll be the victim of your emotions, or someone else's.

We had a buyer, Eric, who was very excited about a sale. He made a full-price offer and was charging full-steam ahead. Then he met with his accountant. Four hours later, he called and said he was out of the deal. He said his accountant had run the numbers and said, "What, are you nuts?" That was the end of it. He had put a lot into getting comfortable with the deal and then the emotion of his accountant killed it. His accountant was right to be skeptical, but if Eric had pulled his accountant in earlier in the process, if he had gathered that data, he could have made the decision to make a counteroffer or restructure the deal. He was fueled by the emotions of the moment and he walked.

You don't want to be a tire kicker and take on too much information and never pull the trigger, but you want good information that you understand and can rely on. You can never have enough information.

Beware the Ego

Ever go to an auction where everyone is bidding? You buy because you don't want to get outbid. And before you know it, you bought something you don't want. You think, "What did I just do?" If your ego's flaring, you're not listening. You're concerned only about yourself. You're not amassing the data that's going to enable you to do a good deal.

We have a longtime client, Mike, who's a master at letting his ego run the show. Everything he does is driven by "I want it. I know what I'm looking at." In truth, he often does know what he's looking at, but the times he didn't have cost him a lot of money. His most recent venture was definitely an ego-driven investment, a sports company, and it's not making money.

Like Mike, many of us get attached to being the smartest person in the room. You might be the smartest person in the room regarding compliance or making birdhouses—whatever your business expertise is—but you are probably not the smartest person in the room when it comes to doing a deal.

Don't Be the Smartest Person in the Room

We worked with Sharon, a computer consultant, who in selling her business wouldn't listen to us as to what the market value was, how to structure the deal, and how to flag the apparent warning signs. Like many of our clients, she'd spent her whole professional life being the smartest person in the room in her day-to-day business. It can be hard for these people to turn that off and leave their egos at the door when there are people in the transaction they should be listening to. In Sharon's case, it cost her dearly. She made a bad deal. You never want to hold on to being the smartest person in the room when there are others around you who are just as smart or smarter. It's a bad way to play cards.

As a buyer, you're coming into the transaction with a

certain amount of confidence in yourself. That's good, because you've got to believe you can make a success of this. But inevitably, the seller is going to irritate you or do something stupid, or we're going to tell you things you don't want to hear. Accept that. Have confidence in the people around you, and don't let the transaction be about you.

Sellers, on the other hand, are likely thinking about what a huge opportunity they're giving you, how lucky you should feel, and how you should give them whatever they want. Buyers are thinking about what needs fixing, how much money they're going to spend, how they're giving the seller this great opportunity to get out. If you allow these mindsets to percolate, they can sabotage everything.

COMMUNICATION, COMMUNICATION, COMMUNICATION

Body Language

Getting in the room with someone can reveal much more than a phone call or an email. We love technology, we're addicted to efficiency, we like to Skype and email. But while being face-to-face might mean a car ride, it can also mean learning a lot from how someone responds to what you say and how they're saying what's on their mind. If someone's got their arms crossed over their chest the whole meeting, you know you're walking down the wrong path. The ability to sit face-to-face can be a key point in negotiating.

We're dealing with an attorney now who's responding to us with emails typed in all caps at ten o'clock at night. It's not helping us get closer to a deal. If she had just picked up the phone and started a dialogue about her concerns, we'd be getting somewhere.

Too much face time can be a liability, but at key stressful points of a negotiation, it can have enormous benefits. When we're sitting with each other, we can have a relationship. It's harder to get mad at someone who's right there in front of you. There's greater respect for each other because we've met, we know what each other looks like, we have a sense of body language, voice, movements.

Often, buyers and sellers don't want to meet. But if a deal's breaking down, we encourage them to sit down together. Nine times out of ten, they come out of the room liking each other and the deal moves forward.

Relationships play a vital part in every negotiation. Structure the deal so it makes sense from a business perspective. But your success in managing the relationships in the transaction is going to have a huge impact on your ability to successfully execute it.

3

PANDORA'S BOX

Instaview founder and CEO Bill McDonald was a renegade. He loved his guns and his bourbon. He also loved his company, which struggled for years until he was finally able to turn the corner and make it a financial success. During those difficult years, a father-and-son team, Jonathan and Rob, worked for him. They became partners with small equity stakes. Johnathan, the father, planned to eventually retire, but he and his son were looking forward to the day when Rob, who was now the company's head of sales, would buy the business from Bill. That plan had always been on the table, fueled by many bourbon-soaked nights, when he and Rob would bat around the transition. They even drew up some basic legal agreements about when Rob could exercise an option.

Rob had spent his whole career with this company and was a big part of its success, but he had no plan as to how he'd run the company or finance the transaction. He was on the West Coast and the company was in New England, but he hadn't even thought about moving. Sales can be done remotely, but you can't run the day-to-day operations of a manufacturing company from afar. When he realized that Rob wasn't planning on moving and wasn't interested in the operational end, Bill lost faith in the transaction.

Bill wanted to step away and engaged us to help move things along. Rob left the company. He was in his mid-thirties and his future had unexpectedly changed. He still had a stake in the company, but his plans to take over had unraveled.

Rob didn't want to move and he didn't want to run a factory, but not all the fault in the failed deal lies with him. Bill had set up the purchase option so that Rob would need a million dollars to buy 12 percent of the company. Rob didn't think the option through. He didn't realize that no bank was going to finance that, but on the other hand, the option Bill offered wasn't a reasonable plan. Bill and Rob had both gotten too comfortable with the "You're going to buy this company!" exclamations that came on their nights out. They'd both failed to create an effective plan for making it happen.

By the time we were brought in to assess the situation, it was too late for Rob. Our engagement was a warning to Rob that all was not as carved in stone as he thought. Several other offers to buy the company had been made by outside buyers. Rob had no way to match them. The relationship became overwhelmed with discomfort and unhappiness; all the good things they'd built up over the years receded into the background.

Rob had been with the company from the start, before it had any real business. He'd built the company's success through his sales success, but ironically, now the company's great valuation was keeping him from owning it. The more successful the business became, the less opportunity he had to own it. Bill could have built a structure and a plan to accommodate Rob, but he didn't.

By the time we were brought in, there was little we could do to help Rob. He left with nothing after ten years of service.

THE UNPREDICTABLE

We were kicked off another transaction after two years of effort because we had an off-the-record conversation with our buyer's wife. Ellie wasn't planning to be hands-on in the business at all, but we always want the spouses on board. We traveled to visit her and take her temperature about the deal. How important was it to her to see it done?

Over a few hours, we learned about her family, her children, how she felt about buying the business—much more and much franker than we'd anticipated. We thought it had been a great success. We were high-fiving each other, celebrating how the end was in sight and how we'd knocked this meeting out of the park. Then her husband went dark on us for a while. He resurfaced, took us to lunch, and fired us. He said he had decided against the deal and picked up the check. We got paid.

What we thought was a great conversation with the wife didn't sit well with the husband. We think that day he heard a lot he'd never heard before, like how dissatisfied his wife was. Because we were very candid with each other, we became a problem for him. All of a sudden, we went from being his allies in the process to his adversaries in achieving his goal.

ARE YOU SURE YOU WANT THAT DRINK?

Bourbon wasn't a part of every meeting with our client Dave, but it contributed to things being said that should have been kept under wraps. After a couple of drinks, promises get made, and you wake up the next morning and you don't remember what those promises were. Dave had been operating like that so long that it was just part of his personality. When you've got a growing business, you might say a few things to key employees whom you're concerned about losing, and then you can't back those things up later. There's a saying: "A sober man's mind is on a drunk man's tongue." If you're trying to initiate or get through a deal, there may be things beneath the surface that are not in your best interests to have come out.

Another longtime client, Peter, is known to start cocktail hour at four in the afternoon. We've grown accustomed to the personality change that happens in him from morning to later in the day, when the emails start flying in. Then, at night, he's angry. The gloves come off. We wake up and spend a good portion of the morning doing damage control, cleaning up after the emails he's sent the night before. It was a long buyout process with him and a partner. We always knew once he'd had a couple of cocktails, things could change in short order.

That said, we've all gotten a little looser after a couple of glasses of wine and maybe said things we regret. You become friendly, have nice conversations with people, and say things you shouldn't. It happens.

SOCIAL BOUNDARIES

Being friendly and respectful during the deal process is a must, but trying to be friends can throw the delicate balance of advisors, family members, employees, and owners out of whack. It can sabotage your strategy. For instance, you might say something at the bar or over dinner that a buyer interprets as "don't worry about it." As your advisors, we do have to worry about it, and whatever you say to the other side can compromise the long game. You might have met them in the past, at conferences and retreats or socially, but do what you can to put that social relationship on hold during the deal. You can resume your friendship after.

Sometimes we might even use the social conflicts to our advantage. We have a buyer and seller right now whom we don't think should be doing a deal together. They won't listen to us, but we've got a feeling that when the spouses meet, everything will fall apart. The buyer and seller are opposites. One's aggressive, overeducated, shoots firsts and asks questions later. The seller is modest and easygoing. We're pretty sure they'll scare the hell out of each other; their oil-and-water temperaments will kill the deal once they meet and their spouses affirm their suspicions.

CUT UP THE NAPKINS

We've all heard stories of successful business plans being sketched out on a cocktail napkin at a hotel bar. Don't do a succession deal on a napkin! That might work when you're going into business, but it doesn't work when you're trying to get out. The buyer picks up the napkin the next morning and says, "Wow. You offered me this much?"

There's no context, just numbers that stick in someone's mind. It's not good business.

We've done approximations of napkin deals on legal pads in the office, where we're all looking at the deal together. That's different than the casual scribbles at the bar or restaurant where you're just not in the mindset to be thinking of the deal's moving parts and consequences.

When you're acquiring or selling, stay off the napkins. And the legal pads. Both can be dangerous.

STARTING THE PROCESS

Ideally, your boss will initiate the transition process by engaging an advisor to examine the feasibility of a sale and walk through all the options. As a key step in this process, the advisor will have a conversation with you as a key employee. It's probably not in anyone's interest to open Pandora's box by announcing the boss is thinking of a sale. What you might hear from the boss is, "I'm working on a succession plan. Will you sit down and talk with our advisor?"

As advisors, we typically interview key personnel, but at first, we're careful to position it in a way that doesn't reveal the intention to sell. After, we go back to the owner and report the feedback.

We might also interview any prospective buyers who've identified themselves to gauge their level of interest. Having us interview the buyers and employees takes all the social pressure off maintaining their relationship with the owner. They know they can be candid with us and we won't reveal anything unnecessarily. An employee might say, "He's a great guy, but I don't want to own his business." It's also a good way to protect the owner's ego. Hiring someone to handle this part increases the chances of making a successful transition.

When an owner approaches you as an employee, it's a big emotional risk. The owner could be met with rejection or ambivalence. It's like asking someone to be a partner in a firm. If they don't leap at the chance and instead say, "I need a few weeks to think about it," that can be heartbreaking.

As an employee, even a longtime valued employee, you might not think that you're considered a potential buyer. You might not even think buying is possible. We had a situation recently where a buyer found a seller, came to the employees, and announced the sale. A key employee was really hurt that he hadn't been given a chance to buy the business. He didn't know the sale was on the horizon; now, his resentment is going to present some challenges to the transaction.

APPROACHING THE SELLER

If you're a buyer wanting to approach an owner, you must have a well-thought-out plan as to why you're the one to be their successor. Don't underestimate the time it takes to create that plan.

The insurance brokerage deal, the complicated father-and-son fair-market transfer we mentioned in chapter 2, started five years before it was completed. We started with the preliminary questions: What are my options? How do we have these conversations with my dad? What might the deal look like? How do I get it financed? Finally, he reached a point where he knew he'd either need to start his own business or buy his dad's. That's when we approached his dad; the son had already done a lot of homework.

BUILDING THE DREAM

How do you start one of the biggest conversations of your life? Again, it starts with homework. A lot of it comes down to knowing the personality of the seller. This is where the personal side of the work comes into play. What are the seller's buttons going to be? Ensuring her legacy? Keeping the family intact? The amount of money on the table? You need to determine what's going to get the seller to the table. What are the points that can make her say this is a conversation worth having?

The owner has likely spent decades building their dream. Now, you have to come in and tell them you are the person to shepherd their dream into the future. They need to know that you love their company so much you want to own it.

For many owners, the business can feel like a child. They've got to know they're leaving it in good hands. That's why they often trust other family members with it first—they know and trust their values. Sellers are driven by a good fit. They want to know you're going to take care of their employees, of their clients. They might not feel they can get that from someone from the outside. If you're an inside buyer, use this to your advantage. Make sure your pitch of the dream includes your understanding and knowledge, how you can take care of the people, the product, and the culture of the company.

As with any big dream, there's a chance it might not work out. Once you put buying on the table, your relationship with the seller changes forever. If it doesn't work out, you have to tolerate a sense of failure. You have to prepare yourself for that.

LET ME THINK ABOUT IT

When approached by key employees about selling, many owners get concerned about keeping the employees happy.

They say, "Oh, yeah. Glad you're interested. I'd love that. Let's see how things work out. Get back to work." It's not as ominous as it sounds. That's actually a hopeful answer, because an owner has to think through a lot.

An appreciative but measured response is what you both want. It's the first step on a journey of exploration—plan, talk, and see where things take you. It might come to nothing. The worst case is when either side feels like they were promised something that is never going to happen. They still have to work side by side after the deal falls apart. Those can be long days. It's not good for the health of the business either. Those key employees are now very uncomfortable and are going to be looking for another job.

How do you know, though, if the other side is stringing you along with their "exploration"? How long is reasonable? As long as there's progress, even if it's slow, things are likely happening in good faith. A little delay is actually good—it gives the buyer some time to put together a team and gather the right information. Closing the deal could take months. It's when you're not seeing progress, when one side is stalling, that you have to ask the difficult questions.

Sellers often hint that they might be thinking of getting out, and that might start the conversation with a potential buyer. They may be getting older. Their health might be deteriorating. They may be tired or having domestic issues.

The seller might hint, "Boy, I'd love to get out of here at some point." That's how the conversation gets going.

But if the owner is too young or simply not interested in letting their baby go, they can still explore bringing in an interested key employee, family member, or even an outsider as a junior partner. This is very common in professional firms, such as accountants and lawyers. It's a great way for key employees to get the equity they want, and as the owner, you can develop a plan for them to buy you out eventually. It gives you a long time, like a long courting period, and then you get married and have the transaction. In the meantime, the junior partners are held captive by golden handcuffs.

There are ways to keep from letting the door close. Offering a stake or partnership to a buyer can be a good pivot if a seller can't close. They can go back to the buyer and say, "I'm not ready" and offer a stake instead. They can say, "What if I bring you on at 10 percent, you buy in, and then we have a plan for you to take over?" That incentivizes everyone to work as partners. This also works for buyers who can't quite get the financing or are starting to realize they don't have the operational knowledge to be the sole owner.

MOVING AHEAD

Starting the exploration for selling can open a Pandora's box of misunderstanding, disappointment, and resentment. Begin the process by assembling a trusted team that can offer you the emotional and practical support to make the best of whatever comes your way.

You might engage experts like us, who can give you ideas on structuring the deal and the company's valuation. You'll also have an accountant and attorney and possibly a banker and financial advisor. Mentors and friends should be relied on, and never underestimate the value of a supportive team at home. Let's take a deeper look at these players and how to assemble the ideal team for your transaction.

TEAM BUILDING

4

As a buyer or a seller, the best thing you can do for yourself is build a good team. Start with finding an experienced advisor with a good track record of facilitating successful business transfers. Someone like us: A firm that has the skills and experience to guide you through the transaction and give you personal attention and support.

If you're hiring mergers and acquisitions guys like us, take a look at how many tombstones they have. How many deals have they closed? Most importantly, ask for references both of professionals they have worked with and, if possible, clients. That should give you an indication of their success.

INSULATING THE BUYER

On occasion, we get engaged to run point on the transaction. We're brought in to keep a tense personal relationship between the buyer and the seller from complicating things. In other words, someone has to be the jerk. Guess who it gets to be?

We have to wear body armor and a hard hat during these meetings, but we also get to see the soft belly. We can take a bad situation and massage it and make it easier for everyone. We're the jerks, but we're also the people who forestall the crises. We blunt the insults and the scars.

We also help build a bridge between the buyer and seller. We can lend an ear and have conversations with them they couldn't have with each other. Then we can soften it and relay it to the other side. We're good at spin.

LEGAL ADVICE

Next, you need a good lawyer. If your legal advice is weak or you have a bad attorney, the deal can fall apart. This happened to us recently with a client, a seller who chose an attorney they had worked with in the past. The problem is that the work the attorney had done for them previously was establishing a family trust. As the deal moved forward, it became very clear to us that they had never handled a single commercial transaction and had a very sketchy knowledge of business law. The attorney tried to cover up their lack of knowledge by doing a lot of ranting and raving about how things were going to be done their way.

That put the buyer off right from the start. But when they spent hours trying to renegotiate the existing letter of intent, which is a nonbinding document, the attorney's lack of knowledge and experience showed. The buyer walked away from the deal. The attorney's behavior wasn't the only reason, but it was a big part of the final decision.

Commercial transactions have a certain flow to them. There are parts you worry about and parts you don't until you need to. And you can only know which parts those are through experience. That's why you need a lawyer who specializes in these types of transactions. Drafting or reviewing asset purchase agreements or stock purchase agreements is tricky; an inexperienced lawyer will miss important points.

A good attorney is going to take advantage of a bad one for the sake of their client. Always start the sale process by getting referrals for an attorney who knows commercial transactions, who practices business law and frequently closes deals. Ask your business associates for recommendations. Ask your bankers—they have a good idea of who's good and who isn't among the local lawyers. With an attorney, you can ask, "How many commercial transactions do you handle a year? How many have you done?

How many different structures and types of transactions?" You'd want to hear, "A lot."

TRANSACTIONS ARE A SPORT—GET THE BEST PLAYERS

Deals come with adrenaline rushes. You want someone who knows how to ride that rush and get the best deal done. As a buyer, you need an attorney who can not only get the deal done but can also find all the skeletons in the closet and read between the lines. If you have a bad attorney, one who's done only divorce work or auto accidents or torts, he'll kill your commercial purchase with his lack of experience.

Ego is another area where attorneys tend to let the process get the better of them. Some get into nitpicking and posturing. Attorneys like this make mountains out of molehills to try and prove they know what they're doing—and collect fees at every six-minute increment.

Interview potential lawyers and make sure you like the person you're going to be sitting across from to do the deal. If you find you made a mistake, fire the attorney.

ACCOUNTANTS

We pick on lawyers, but accountants often cause problems

as well. When you're building your team, make sure the accountant has experience with business transactions. In our experience, most accounting firms don't handle business transactions. They have as much a chance of destroying a deal as a bad attorney. We've often had to deal with inexperienced accountants who hold on tight to their excessive valuations, unfair allocations, and bad advice. When allocating the purchase price of a deal, it has to be driven by tax law, tax advantages, and tax wisdom. If your accounting firm struggles with that, you can get into real difficulties.

OTHER ADVISORS

Other team members you might engage include financial advisors and commercial bankers. In our opinion, financial advisors have a lot of long-term value but may not add a lot initially to the deal. From a deal perspective, they may be able to counsel you on the status of the company's 401(k) plan, the benefits package, and some other items that might come up in due diligence, but where their value will really shine through is in helping you leverage the money you do make into other investments so you're diversified. One reason many owners need to get a higher price than what the business is worth is because they were never proactive in investing outside of the business. It can be a little painful today, but the long-term payoff of having a good financial advisor on your team is huge.

If you're the buyer, a commercial banker can take a quick look at the deal and tell you what they feel the bank or the general market is going to accept in terms of risk, rates, and terms. Financing specialists, such as experts from the SBA, or development or manufacturing specialists can help you understand what exactly you're buying and how to finance it.

We've started using insurance specialists more and more. They can assess the risk of the acquisition from the property and casualty perspective, look at the risk from the benefits package, and identify where skeletons may be lying in wait. If it's a large acquisition, at least large in terms of number of employees, we like to bring in an HR specialist to do due diligence, access the HR files, and identify where the pitfalls may be.

We also highly recommend IT specialists for due diligence. You need someone to go in and take a look at the network, hardware, and software and tell you what needs work and where things could go wrong. Today, technology is a huge part of any acquisition.

We also might use a real estate specialist if there's real estate involved.

Tracking down qualified, experienced people with expertise in your industry can be a lot of work. That's why locating the right specialists for you is one of the most important things we do.

WHO'S IN YOUR FOXHOLE?

You need friends and family around you during the deal. You need people who have your best interests at heart, who aren't worried about maximizing their fees or notching up another deal. But a word of caution—don't use friends and family as deal advisors if they don't have experience in deals. You need people who will help you see the bigger goal when you get cold feet or get hung up on details that aren't worth it. If they don't have the expertise, they should be there for emotional support and a sanity check on how the decisions will impact you and your family.

Both sides need good teams. If a seller has a bad team, that becomes the buyer's problem, and vice versa. As a buyer, if you see the seller has put together a bad team and is dead set on listening to them, bring your concerns to the forefront: "Your lawyer's delaying, your accountant doesn't know what he's doing, your financial advisor's an idiot." Of course, do it more tactfully than that, because the seller chose those people to be on his team. You don't want to insult his judgment.

When we have to work with bad teams, we try to be patient and walk clients through things. We try to help everyone stay cool and calm and work through the problems. But sometimes the tensions can become unbearable, and the deal falls apart.

HIDDEN AGENDAS

The problem we often have with seller teams is that the lawyers and accountants and other advisors don't really want the sale to go through. If it does, then they lose a client. They're not deliberately trying to sabotage the deal, but it can be hair-raising when you know you're losing a lucrative client through the sale. It can make you less cooperative, less fast on your feet. It's often subconscious, especially on large accounts that you know you can't replace.

How can you know the people on your team have your best interests at heart? You should get a feeling early on, in those first conference calls. As advisors, we've got a good sense of who's likely to be reasonable and who's likely to throw fits and tantrums.

THE ESSENTIAL TEAM

To recap, these are the major players on a good team and how they add value to the transaction.

MERGERS AND ACQUISITIONS EXPERTS

We're often referred to as deal advisors. This role is often overlooked, but it's incredibly valuable to have someone who's focused just on the deal. We're currently representing a buyer who's an employee and we have a counterpart on the seller's side. It's great because we speak the same language and share the same objective: their client wants to sell to our client. There's a lot of benefit to having us involved.

ATTORNEY

Attorneys offer advice, draft documents, follow up on them, and then handle the closing. They create pre-closing agendas, complete closing work, and take care of post-closing efforts. Anyone with transactional experience tends to do a good job. Attorneys also handle the regulatory filings.

To save costs, most of our clients keep attorneys out of non-binding documents, such as letters of agreement. It's expensive and unnecessary to have an attorney execute these. Attorneys are there to capture the legal parts of the deal.

TAX ACCOUNTANT

Anyone can file a tax return with some degree of competence, but a tax accountant understands all the complexities of structuring a transaction and its tax impact. The tax consequences to the buyer and seller on a stock deal or an asset deal are very different. The tax accountant is there to advise you on structuring the deal from a tax standpoint.

FINANCIAL ADVISOR

A good financial advisor looks at the bigger picture and helps you plan now for what you'll do later, when you need to find ways to invest the profits from the business.

COMMERCIAL BANKER

We're not talking about your standard branch manager here. You must make sure you're dealing with a commercial banker. That can be hard with some of the bigger banks. Sometimes they won't let you reach up to that level. They might say, "This is only a half-million-dollar deal and it's got to come up through the branch manager." You don't want that kind of bank.

A community bank is often better equipped to deal with smaller transactions. Credit unions don't tend to do commercial deals but are a good source if they do. Shop around and find the bank that will let you do business with a commercial specialist.

CREATE LASTING RELATIONSHIPS

If you're the lawyer on a deal and your client buys the company, well, your client's going to need a lawyer in the future. That can become a lasting relationship. M&A guys like us, who advise on deals, often become the people a business relies on for ongoing advice and other deals. We love that—we love to help a business grow and deal with challenges. Commercial bankers are tapped for lines of credit and other financial services.

Make sure your team members have your best interests at heart. It all comes down to hiring good people who know what they're doing.

Once you've assembled a good team, you can take the next steps in the acquisition process. Patience will be required.

PART II

ADVANCE

5

THE PROCESS

A buyer absolutely must take the time to understand the entire process and the realities of the deal. If you don't, the process can collapse quickly. We recently consulted on the financing of a sale of a company that's a bit beyond the start-up stage. The borrower in the deal had trouble understanding that banks have certain parameters for lending. They don't care if you're spending a million dollars to upgrade a piece of real estate. If those upgrades provide an appraised value of only $500,000, that's all they can lend against. You need to understand hard realities like that and how to work with them.

In addition to understanding the deal, you also need to have patience for the process and be willing to take it all in—the good, the bad, the indifferent. You have to check your ego at the door and you have to be willing to pay the market value for getting the deal done.

Buyers without understanding, buyers without patience, buyers with big egos, and buyers who don't want to pay for the deal are all telltale signs that the deal isn't going to come together.

SETTING EXPECTATIONS

If you're going to get what you want in the deal as a buyer, you've got to set your expectations early. The seller likely already has his expectations, and although they're probably higher than what the market value is, that's to be expected. You're the one who has to work hard to get your expectations to match reality.

Buyers' expectations can be tricky. You might be thinking you're just going to buy the business and make a ton of money, or that you can easily run the business better than the next guy, or "Hey, let's buy six of these businesses!" We commonly find that a buyer's expectations are way off the charts. We gently try to bring them down to earth. The goal is for the buyer to find out what the seller wants and see if they can reach an agreement without spending a lot of time and money in the middle.

We represented a buyer in a transaction where the seller had decided that she needed to get cash at the closing. The buyer, her employee, didn't have any cash and was unlikely to be able to borrow any. There was a big gap in their expectations. To bridge it, we talked to the seller's advisor and explained the circumstances—there could be no cash at the closing. If his seller couldn't accept that, the deal was off. Once both parties knew the other's expectation and reality, the deal collapsed. Because the gap between the seller and the buyer was clear, at least it ended quickly and amicably.

Sellers often think things are going to be easy because they've paved a pathway for the deal. After all, the buyer is a family member or loyal employee. We're all in agreement, right? In truth, we're always having to make it clear to both the buyer and seller that even though you want to be on the same page with each other, doing the deal is not necessarily going to be easy, quick, and smooth. Bumps and challenges will always arise.

Whenever we hear, "Oh, this should be an easy deal" (we hear that just about every time), or "We should be able to fly through this deal," or "I shouldn't have any problem getting this financed," we know it's time to readjust expectations. We say, "Wait a minute. If those are your expectations, you shouldn't be looking at this particular deal. They're never easy."

Each side has reasons behind their expectations, which is why we always spend an hour or two on the front end of the deal talking about expectations and getting both sides on the same page.

Sometimes the expectation gap can be a negotiating tactic. Knowing who the seller really is will help you understand if an objection is just posturing or genuinely is a potential deal killer.

A few years ago, we had a good-sized deal where everyone's expectations moved around on the chessboard several times. We spent more time on managing and adjusting expectations than we did on doing the deal. We thought we were going into a relatively easy succession plan: two of the firm's partners were aging out of the firm and selling to the two younger partners. But we ended up spending 75 percent of our time aligning expectations, discussing future performance, past histories, rehashing every deal the firm had ever done—it became very emotional. The sellers were using this approach to drive up the price on the buyers. By pointing out the perceived inadequacies of the buyers, the sellers were establishing that this was a risky proposition that should have a greater premium for them. It was disingenuous, but not everyone plays fair in deals.

VALUATION

Most valuations of businesses use a definition of value

known as "fair market value," which is an Internal Revenue Service standard. The standard assumes that a hypothetical buyer and hypothetical seller are both aware of all the facts of the transaction and neither one has a need to do the transaction. It's a great way to look at things, at least on paper. When we're valuing a business for a transaction, we're no longer dealing with hypothetical buyers and sellers. We're dealing with two parties in real life who need to complete a transaction. Reality needs to usurp the hypothetical.

The reality is, in most cases we have a buyer who can't afford to buy the company at market value with conventional methods. They just don't have the money. They don't have the wherewithal or the assets to buy the company. Perhaps they can borrow part of the asking price, but the seller is going to have to participate to get the deal done.

Buyers and sellers simultaneously overestimate and underestimate each other. A neutral third party can establish fair value that reflects the realities of the circumstances and the market. With that information, both can now get real and do the deal in the context of the circumstances on either side.

INSIGHT AND EXPERIENCE

Both sides can benefit from the insight of advisors who've done multiple deals, who can guide them through taking advantage of the personalities and personal needs present in each transaction. We see a lot of cases where the players can leverage personal insight and experience into favorable terms.

Odd Deals

A lot of deals have twists and turns to them, nuances that need the sort of special attention an experienced professional can help you navigate. These can be the result of money, relationships, financing, or the particular industry involved. In privately held businesses, odd deals often turn up. You can deduct all sorts of things as expenses, for example, and the seller might have been deducting some expenses that surprise you. Employees might have negotiated side deals for perquisites that you'll only discover when you're expected to retain them. All sorts of irregularities that aren't conventional to a third-party sale show up when it's a family or employee sale. You need to have someone who's aware of the possibility of irregularities and can respond to the unexpected.

The True Self

Insider buyers can often use their knowledge of the true

self of the seller to their advantage. After working with someone for a long time, you often understand them more than they understand themselves. You can anticipate their actions before they even occur. That gives you a tremendous opportunity to maximize your position.

Under the Influence

A buyer does well to understand who has the greatest influence over the seller. In one of our deals, an owner was dragging his feet on the financing terms. The buyer had his wife make a passing comment to the owner's wife about the pace of the transaction. The next day, the issue was resolved. It turns out, the owner's wife was the driving force behind the transaction. She didn't want to spend another winter in New England!

Predicting Personality

With experience, we've gotten to know how the other side is likely to react in certain situations. In one deal, we had an owner who was a bully and liked to roll out the tough guy act. However, he'd fold as soon as there was any pushback, because he hated confrontation. Our buyer let the owner bully his way through issues that weren't that important to him, but he prevailed on the point most critical to him. The owner didn't have the stomach to fight and consented to the buyer's demands.

We've seen that response often—bullies in particular are very predictable.

Insider Knowledge

We once had a deal where the seller was playing hardball on the last deal point and threatened to kill the whole transaction over this issue. The buyer was an insider, and he knew that the owner had just accepted an offer on his house and put down a deposit on his retirement home. With that knowledge, he held firm on his position, well aware that the owner was too far into the deal to lose a closing over the last remaining point.

You can never be too aware of all the moving parts of a transaction. Things will change as the deal changes, and it's important to manage your expectations accordingly.

6

SET EXPECTATIONS

When we do deals, we encounter the same set of unrealistic expectations over and over. They're predictable, even among buyers and sellers who are experienced businesspeople. These people would easily recognize unrealistic expectations if they were outsiders observing a deal, but when it comes to their own business, they often can't see them. That's a good reason for bringing in an outside advisor—we can give you a reality check.

THE CURSE OF UNIQUENESS

The most common unrealistic expectation we see is overestimating the uniqueness of the business. Recently, we valued the business of a seller. We told him the price we were putting it on the market for and the offers we expected to get. Sure enough, once it was listed, we got an offer exactly where we expected.

And what did he say? "Not enough." He said, "I've been investing in this business for years and you can't just find one of these businesses anywhere!"

The deal was great. It was better than what he should have expected. But he was driven by his conviction that his business was unique and therefore worth more than what the market will bear. It's very challenging to change a seller's perceptions. It's a frequent occurrence for us to have sellers who are unrealistic about the value of their business. At least they know who to blame—it's always their advisor's fault!

BLIND TO FLAWS

Owners often refer to their businesses as their children or their mistresses. Many work sixty, seventy, eighty hours a week and spend more time with their business than with their families. We've never worked with a seller who didn't gloss over his business's flaws. We've done it ourselves with our own businesses! It's like having a house on the market and there's water in the cellar, but all you say is, "We've had some damp moments..."We all do it when we're selling something or in relationships, just to varying degrees.

Typically, it's part of the buyer's due diligence to find those flaws and address them. I've never met a seller who doesn't say, "Oh, that's not a problem. Don't worry about that. It's easy to fix; only a few dollars to fix it—don't worry about it! It's never been a problem for me."

PAY ME FOR THE PRIVILEGE

Sellers often want a premium for the special opportunity they're giving you to buy their business. They imagine there are so many things you could do with it, it's just primed for greater success if only someone had just a little bit more money and energy to put into it.

They might say, "If I was going to stay longer, I'd do this and this, or if I still had the passion for the business, I'd do that." If, if, if. Buyers think, "Like hell! I'm not paying you for an opportunity. I'm buying a business!" In his mind, the seller is imagining all the things he could do that would make the business worth more, and you'll have the opportunity to do them. But he should have done those things already. You're going to pay only so much for an intangible opportunity.

We were valuing a restaurant recently and things didn't add up. The owner said, "You have some questions."

We said, "Yeah, we got your tax returns. You showed eleven thousand last year for your salary on one million in revenue. But then there's another sheet that shows owner's costs and it says you made sixty grand. What's going on?"

He said, "Well, there's a lot of cash in the business."

Great. We said, "We can't value that." In businesses that take in a lot of cash, this sort of skimming is common. The problem is, you can't finance that. A buyer won't pay for that, in most cases. And sooner or later, the government gets their take, too. The only way to sell is to take a reduced price, so you don't get what you could have. The alternative is to fix your books and get what you're asking, but sooner or later it shows up. And while the IRS doesn't often compare those figures, they can.

YOU CAN KEEP YOUR HISTORY

Sellers often overestimate the extent to which buyers are interested in the history of their business. Sellers love to walk them through how the business was born, how he bought it, how he used to work Saturday afternoons until four o'clock, how he brought his kids up in the business...and on and on. The buyer listens to this and thinks, "Get all that behind me! This is what *I'm* going to do with the business." As a buyer, you're not interested in the fact that the business did ten million in revenue five years ago. You want to know why it's doing only four million now.

There's no question that the history of the business is important. If you're buying Coca-Cola or McDonald's, it's extremely important. But in most cases, get the history and move on. You're going to get bored real fast with the stories of the past.

FAIR MARKET VALUE DOESN'T APPLY

Ultimately, something's only worth what someone will pay for it, no matter what the fair market value is. The buyer says, "This is what I can afford and this is what I think it's worth." That's the reality. If you're an insider buyer, your ability to pay is probably less than an outsider's.

When you're buying real estate or other tangible assets, it's easier to focus on the fair market value. When you're buying a business, determining the fair market value is more challenging, because some of the value is intangible goodwill. You can't argue much about the price on a piece of real estate or a piece of equipment or a vehicle, because in most cases the comparisons are well established. On goodwill, though, battles over fair market value can arise.

An example of this is a project we're working on to facilitate a deal between two partners in a brokerage. One partner is interested in buying out the other. The partner who's leaving got a valuation for the brokerage of $350,000. The other asked us to look at it. When he asked us what we thought the business was worth, we had to say, "Probably nothing."

In this case, there's a huge gap between the practical value and the perceived value. We're saying it's worth nothing. Who's going to buy a company where there are only two employees and the business runs on their institutional knowledge? The fair market is looking at a hypothetical buyer and seller. The valuation equation has multiples and cash flows and rules of thumb. It's great to have that, but can you get that on the open market? No. A buyer says, "I don't necessarily care how you determine the value. This is what I'm willing to pay for it."

SELLER FINANCING

As a buyer, you probably want the seller to finance the deal, or at least a good chunk of it. From the seller's perspective, that's adding insult to injury. Still, seller financing is a common practice. The company might sell for one million, but it's not all cash up front. You might give the seller $800,00 in cash and have them hold $200,000 in your notes and paper for a period. As the buyer, your thinking is, if the seller has faith in their company and in you, they should be willing to finance a part of the deal.

The seller says, "I just want to go to Florida. I don't want to hold your risky paper." You, the buyer, want to see a little faith. The banks do, too. They prefer seller financing because it reduces their risk. The seller stays behind the banks when it comes to financing.

OVERANALYZING THE TRANSACTION

You do your gut checks and you listen to your instincts, but if you're a buyer not used to buying, it's easy to over-analyze the deal and look to find a way out. You might get hung up on noncritical items. You lose focus on why you thought that it was a good business or a good industry to be in. Instead, you get all caught up on little items that turn bad. Overanalysis leads to paralysis and that becomes your way out.

THE OPPORTUNITY IS THEIRS FOR THE TAKING

As a buyer, you recognize that you're taking a huge risk. You're not going to pay a premium, because you've got a lot of work to do with the business to improve it. The seller still thinks you should pay a high price. You respond, "I'll pay you for what you built, but I'm not going to pay for the future. I'm the one who has to do that work. I have to take the risk."

There's a way to bridge the gap: Let the seller have some participation in the future. It's called an earnout. If the company is supposed to take in $2 million a year and actually does $2.2 million, the deal with the buyer may let him pick up a portion of that for two or three years. Buyers like the earnout, because it's only paid if the company reaches the performance target. Sellers like it, because it gives them the opportunity to make a little bit more money, particularly if they are confident in the business's ability to perform. We use it frequently to bridge the gaps between the buyer and seller.

MONEY

When we're engaged, whether for the seller or buyer, the first question we ask is, what is the client's perspective of value? What do they need from the deal? That's important. We need to know what your expectations are around value, what does the structure need to be, are you willing to take money over time? What are your requirements? All those things come into the financial drives of the deal. No matter what a seller tells you, the reason most of them are selling is because they need to cash out. Sometimes the decision's driven by legacy or wanting to help others, but ultimately, it's got to make sense for them financially.

PERSONAL ISSUES

A seller may have health issues, domestic issues, or limitations as to what they can do with the company. They could be very, very tired. Maybe they've been in it way too long.

A lot of times, personal issues make the owner decide to sell. The buyer has to recognize the issues and either play up or down to them. In our experience, personal issues drive as much or more of the process as money issues.

On the other hand, if you're the buyer, you want to know if they're committed to selling to you. What level of commitment do you need to start this process? Also, are you sure the seller can actually let go? There's a lot of emotion tied up in their business. For buyers, can they accept the change in lifestyle, the risk, and the potential failure? Fear of failure drives a lot of us to ultimately not take risks.

Buyers hope to expand the business. They think about legacy, too. They think about how much better it would be to control their own destiny instead of work on the clock every day for someone else. Buyers and sellers usually have this in common. If the seller goes back to when he started the business, it's usually the same reasons as the buyer's desire to own. The buyers are looking to set their families up and make a good living doing something for themselves.

THE DEAL STRUCTURE

The deal structure is challenging, because what's good for the buyer isn't good for the seller, and vice versa. We tell our sellers, "It's not what you sell for. It's what you get." With the buyers, we say, "It's not what you pay for. It's what you get."

One of our recent deals was for a company in the software space. The company had no assets whatsoever—the value was all in goodwill. The seller wanted a stock sale, however, which doesn't allow for amortization of the price. We had structured our offer to the seller to try to account for the tax implications of that, because as an intangible asset, goodwill can be amortized over up to fifteen years, which beats zero in a stock deal. The purchase price was $7 million, higher than the buyer planned to pay. The ability to get a tax write-off using a faster method to offset the cost of paying so much money made it worthwhile. The structure here became extremely important.

BE CAUTIOUS

Understand the risks you're taking. If there are bumps or fails, what have you put at stake? Have you brought a spouse into the deal? Have you risked family assets? Evaluate the risks.

Is there a sacred cow inside the deal? What are the things that we need an extra layer of sensitivity in addressing? Perhaps it's a relationship with a longtime employee or a vendor. Or maybe family members have to be kept on the payroll after the business changes hands.

In one recent deal, the seller wanted assurances that the buyers were going to give employment contracts to his children. The buyer wanted to talk to the kids first, but the seller didn't want to tell his kids the firm was being sold. Not surprisingly, the buyers balked and the deal fell through.

EXPECT TO BE SURPRISED

Generally, these issues don't impact the terms of the deal or the way you operate the company after the transaction is completed. It's more about being proactive and understanding items that may create unexpected conflict in the future.

As a buyer, don't be surprised if the owner has questions for you about many of these issues as well. Answer the questions posed to you in the same manner you would a job interview. Be honest, but don't give away too much information. Craft your answers to be respectful of the owner's responses, but at the same time, be somewhat noncommittal to any definitive answers. You won't gain anything by putting all your cards on the table at this point. You don't want to kill the deal before it gets started.

The deal depends on both parties agreeing about the assessed value of the company. That agreement can be hard to reach.

7

VALUE ASSESSMENT

We once had a client who was looking at a strategic acquisition. They asked us to look at the value of the business. We came back with a number that was quite a bit below what the seller was asking. The asking price was $5.5 million, but our value was in the neighborhood of $2.5 million. The seller wasn't too happy with this and asked us to explain how we had come with a value so different from theirs.

We put together an abbreviated summary—we didn't want to give them too much inside information on what we did! Their appraiser, a veteran in the field, came back and blasted us: "You didn't use the right database! You also used these stupid rules of thumb as part of your equation. We call them the 'rules of dumb.'" He went on and on, giving us a real earful. But at the end of the day, he never considered the buyer's perspective, market conditions, and most importantly, the realities of the company. In fact, the company had only one customer and their contract was set to expire the following year. There wasn't much in the way of value beyond fixed assets and some limited goodwill. Facing reality can be hard for a seller.

To establish a value for the business, buyers and sellers frequently engage an appraiser. Appraisers generally value a company utilizing the IRS definition of fair market value, which is defined as a hypothetical buyer and a hypothetical seller, neither of whom have the requirement to act and have no relevant knowledge of the facts surrounding the company. To arrive at their opinion of value, an appraiser will use a number of methods such as the Income Approach, which considers the value of the company based on future cash flows. However, when contemplating a transaction, it's critical that the appraiser take into consideration the market realities.

THE SCIENCE AND ART OF VALUATION

Certified appraisers are frequently engaged to value businesses for a variety of purposes: estate planning, divorces, tax cases, and the like. When valuing a business, they have a set of methods, processes, and guidelines that they're required to follow. This uniformity makes a lot of sense for many purposes, but it can miss the mark if the methodology they apply isn't practical or appropriate for the realities of a particular company, or if it doesn't consider the value from a transaction perspective.

We were recently engaged to provide an opinion of the value of a company in a partnership dispute. Both sides engaged an advisor to determine a fair and equitable value to dissolve the partnership. We were engaged by the partner who wanted to exit and arrived at a value in the $500,000 range. The certified appraiser on the other side said it had no value and was adamant in defense of his opinion, arguing about capitalization rates and other details. Our client eventually bought the business for a number closer to what we had identified. He recognized the market value and opportunity of the company. The business is doing better than ever.

THE LIMITS OF SCIENCE

Certified appraisers have a strong knowledge of the science of valuation. That's what they're licensed in, what they went to school for, and why they can hang out their shingle. They invest a lot of time and money on their licenses and accreditations from the American Society of Valuation, the Institute of Business Appraisers, the American Institute of Certified Public Accountants (AICPA), and others.

Certified appraisals have their place, especially in big

deals. We don't think they're as useful in small market deals, because valuing a smaller company for a transaction requires not only the science but some art. Less skilled appraisers don't like to bring the art into it too often.

The art is understanding what's going on in the market, how the deal is going to be structured, and how it's going to be financed. The art is also knowing what the buyer is going to pay for it, not what the seller or appraiser thinks it's worth. The art comes in answering the question, "What are the buyers paying for that opportunity?" The answer evolves constantly, so we evolve with it. A business might have a value of a 5X multiple today and next year have a multiple of 4X. The business didn't change, but the market did.

Both sides in a transaction should invest in appraisals of the business, but they shouldn't be treated as gospel. They're important, because if they're reasonable, they provide a baseline for negotiation. However, whenever a seller shouts about what the valuation said, we always remind them that by definition, the valuation assumes the parties are hypothetical. And once we have a real buyer and a real seller, things are no longer hypothetical.

THE VALUE OF ART

The art side is really about taking the buyer's perspective into the valuation. Buyers consider the impact of management teams, customer types and concentrations, industry verticals, and other intangibles when valuing a company. These evaluations impact the multiples that are applied to the cash flow. The multiples can be a bit of a guess, because they are frequently buyer-specific. In determining the value, it's critical to understand what impacts the multiple and how it applies to the company.

We all apply the same method, but we have different approaches to it. We might apply a multiple of 4.5X, while a different appraiser applies a multiple of 5.25X. Why the difference? Opinions differ, and so does the data we look at to support them. We happen to be market-driven. We use data that tells us what the market's doing, such as sales of similar companies. While we place a greater emphasis on this, other appraisers may not.

Industry specifics are also an important part of the intangible aspects of a valuation. Sometimes appraisers don't know a lot about the specific industry, and that can hurt the process badly. One example we see often is in the insurance industry, where appraisers include contingency and bonus payments in the valuation as part of the cash flow. We have to point out that these are one-time events that may or may not occur. They have to be treated differently from the recurring revenue derived from commissions.

Another challenge in valuations is the impact of historical performance. Past performance is great for context, but just because a company did X dollars of business two years ago doesn't mean it's a reasonable proxy for the future. We're less interested in how the company has historically performed than we are with present trends and the near-term prospects. Buyers frequently focus on the Trailing Twelve Months (TTM) performance, because it provides a rolling look at what's happening with the business. Valuations that don't take into consideration recent performance should be considered suspect.

Ideally, a seller's appraiser shares how he got to his number with the buyer and his advisors. Sellers are usually eager to share valuations they're happy with—they want to put them in the buyer's face. The buyer is very likely going to have another opinion. And if a buyer has a valuation that's much less than what the seller is anticipating, it makes sense for the buyer to say, "Look, this is what our people came up with, and here are the reasons why." Then you try to find a middle ground, or you disengage.

OFF THE MARK

Appraisers can miss the mark when they're using bad data or making bad assumptions. They might be using the discounted cash flow method of valuation and applying growth rates that aren't sustainable. They could be applying a capitalization rate that is too aggressive or one that's not aggressive enough. They could be looking at the wrong data set when they look at transactional multiples. There are many, many bad assumptions you can make when you start to do a valuation. We once came across a situation where the seller was valuing his single jewelry store with $350,000 in revenue, based on the multiples of publicly traded jewelry chains. Needless to say, his store wasn't going to sell for 17X its revenue.

A common error we see is appraisers who are overaggressive in evaluating the true cash flow, the company's discretionary cash flow. Another we see is being too aggressive with the multiple they're applying. This can come from a basic lack of awareness or laziness, the common mistakes of human nature. They might not be digging that deeply into the company. Or they may be, but beauty is in the eye of the beholder. Most valuation engagements are occupied with the process and method to apply a valuation, not the depth of the research. Again, they are using a hypothetical context and may not be looking at it from the same lens that the buyer is.

THE JUSTIFICATION PURCHASE TEST

The justification purchase test is a mechanism used to determine if the deal could be financed conventionally. Based on a certain amount of capital, can you go to the bank or the seller and put down 20 percent and borrow the remaining 80 percent? What can you afford in debt service? As an individual buyer, you can't pay more than what you can finance. Strategic buyers and financial buyers who don't need to worry about the financing component can pay a lot more. A bank isn't going to lend you money if you can't make the debt payments and meet debt service coverage ratios. They'll also want to make sure that what's left to you after debt service is enough for you to still generate profits.

We recently valued a company for a partnership dispute. The multiples, based on the size of the company, should have been around 3.5X or 4X, which is what the selling partner expected. We ran the justification purchase test, and it failed. Using the multiples, the company should have had a value of about $600,000, but according to the justification purchase test, it was valued at about $350,000. The seller recognized the flaw in their logic and we were able to come up with a more realistic purchase price.

PAYING EXTRA FOR WHAT YOU CAN'T AFFORD

Sometimes you stretch your offer. Sometimes you find a way to acquire something that you can't quite afford on paper. There may be reasons to do this, or you may figure out a way to borrow more or restructure the deal. You may arrange to get more equity to change the equation.

For instance, you're buying a new car. You look at something for $40,000, when based on what you can afford, you should only be looking at something at $35,000. In the long run, you think the extra $5,000 is worth it, because you want it and you need it. It makes sense to you. You're going to stretch yourself a bit, even though it's not quite in your budget, to come up with the extra $50 a month.

We come to that crossroads in human nature all the time. It's more than what you can afford, but you want it, so you'll stretch. When you're buying a business, that means coming up with your own capital, because the bank isn't going to stretch. Typically, a bank is not going to finance something you can't afford. We've stretched ourselves a few times; so have our clients. You have to ask yourself how much of a sacrifice you're willing to make.

FAIR MARKET VALUE AND THE IRS

IRS Revenue Ruling 59-60 is the basis of virtually all appraisals. It defines "fair market value" as the selling price between a hypothetical buyer and a hypothetical seller who are both aware of all the relevant facts and neither are under the obligation to buy or sell. That's the standard for appraisals. It's the standard if you're valuing something for an estate, but it's not the standard when you're dealing with an actual transaction.

When you're valuing from a market perspective, there's a definition called Fair Value, which is a standard set by the International Private Equity and Venture Capital Association (IPEV). Fair Value is calculated by taking fair market value and considering the market conditions. Market conditions could move your multiples up or down, or they could be affected by a recent transaction in the company. Fair Value has a lot of different angles to consider from the buyer's perspective.

ASSET CHANGES

The value can also change as the assets change. Once you've determined the value, you add certain assets to it. You may add the cash the company will keep after a sale or from receivables due from customers that aren't going to be included in the sale. Then you subtract the items you're going to have to pay off before the sale, such as bank loans from the owners. Asset values can change quite a bit.

If you're looking to retain those assets and pay off those liabilities and they change dramatically, that can change your overall valuation of what a seller is going to get or what a buyer is going to have to pay for it.

These things typically affect our valuations when we update them throughout the process. It obviously can affect the deal as you get closer to closing. Post-closing issues also affect the valuation, because often when you acquire a company, you set escrows: certain standards that can't be determined until 90 or 120 days after the closing. These adjustments might be for working capital or the collection of receivables. Post-closing adjustments can change the valuation from what it was at the actual closing.

PLAYING IT OUT

In a real-life transaction, the buyer and seller are either going to agree to the value or not. If the buyer's not comfortable with it, he's going to go get his own appraisal in order to look at it from his perspective. If both parties are reasonably comfortable with the valuation, you start the negotiation from that perspective.

Sometimes that goes very smoothly. We did a valuation for a deal from the buyer's side and the seller just accepted it, without doing their own. They said, "You know, that's exactly where we were thinking. We can work within this number." Most deals involve at least a little disagreement. If you strongly disagree with a valuation, you may want to engage someone to review it. But if you're very far apart, there's little reason to spend any more time or money. The fees for certified appraisers start at $5,000 or $10,000. Transaction advisors like us, who look at the deal from a market or buyer's perspective, are more in the range of $3,000 to $5,000.

FINDING AN APPRAISER

Typically, bankers, accountants, and lawyers will recommend appraisers they've worked with locally. It's easier to find real estate appraisers than business appraisers. It's a small world. You can search on the web, but a private referral is preferable.

We offer valuations as part of our services. We won't sell a business until we've come to a consensus with the seller and we're both on the same page on the value. If we're not, we're going to waste a lot of time and money.

We don't represent buyers without having an idea of what the justification for them to buy is, how much money they have, and how much financing they can get. Otherwise, we've got a waste of time there as well.

On occasion, we don't go through with the appraisal process. When the seller is being reasonable and is probably going to finance the entire purchase, there's no reason to spend money on an appraisal. If the deal is friendly and everyone's comfortable that this isn't an arm's-length transaction, you can let it go. If everyone is on the same page and can look at how the value was arrived at and the lawyers are happy, you don't need to pay for a valuation.

A valuation is a critical starting point for negotiating the deal. Once it's achieved, the important work of facing up to the realities of the deal begins. It's now time to get the buyer's and seller's interests to align.

8

NEW REALITIES

On occasion, we'll encounter a deal where what the buyer wants and the seller needs are never going to align. However, if the parties really want to make it happen, we can usually find a way to bridge the gap. The deal we arranged for Jim and his dad, Eli, is a good example.

Jim went to work for his father soon after graduating from college. He wasn't sure he wanted to work in the family business but thought he would give it a shot. At first, Eli thought Jim would be working for him for just a short time. He thought it might be a patch before he found his true career.

It turned out that Jim loved his work and became highly engaged in the business. He began estimating the jobs and discovered he had a talent for it. Eli soon promised that down the line, he would own part of the company and own all of it after he retired.

At that point, they came to us to discuss the buy-in options. We set up an arrangement that had Jim buy in over five years. He bought 10 percent a year for four years, and then on the fifth year, he bought 9 percent. He now owned 49 percent of the business. When Eli was ready to retire, he would sell the other remaining 51 percent at a discount. Everything was going along fine, until retirement time arrived and Jim wanted to exercise his option on the remaining 51 percent. By then, Eli's lifestyle had inflated. He and his wife had bought a beautiful home in Charleston and loved the warmer winters. They had a much more lavish lifestyle than what they had been accustomed to when Eli made the agreement with Jim. They needed money.

The money his parents would get when Jim bought Eli out now wasn't enough. We had to climb over that hurdle by reminding Eli that he had made the deal with Jim, that he had paid for the first 49 percent, and Jim was exercising his option.

The first new reality was that Eli's reality had changed; Jim's hadn't. This wasn't a case of their saying, "We think the business is worth more." This was the deal, in writing, that had been agreed to.

The next new reality was with Jim. Not only was he ready financially and professionally to buy the business, but when he acquired the 51 percent of the business, he became the real owner, the CEO. He expected to be treated as such.

His parents had a hard time letting go and respecting the boundaries. We helped them accept the new realities, but it was a struggle. On this deal, we were as much family therapists as deal experts. The annual family picnic hasn't been the same since, but it's getting better.

THE BIGGER PICTURE

We had a client, a company started by two brothers and a cousin decades ago, that became fairly successful. Over the years, the first generation brought eight of their children into the business. There were countless other children of the founders who didn't join the business. The eight cousins grew the business to the point where they were running the operations and driving the company to incredible growth and profits. When it came to big decisions, now eleven people were at the table providing their opinions on the business strategy and operations.

For more than a decade, the family had been talking about succession plans. Several firms like ours had tried, at considerable expense to the company, to find a way for the first generation to hand the company over to the second generation. It always failed. We were brought in for another try. What we discovered once we were hired is that they didn't want to give up the benefits of ownership even though all of them were approaching their seventies and at varying levels of activity in the business. When it came time to structure a deal, they placed too much emphasis on their past contributions to the current success, which skewed their perception of the value. They didn't want to acknowledge the impact of the second generation on the business and the challenges they were dealing with as the business grew. Most importantly, they didn't recognize that because of the nature of the business, the only buyer for the business was the second generation. No one outside the family was going to buy the business unless those family members stayed involved.

The second generation, now in their thirties and forties, was willing to be fair, but they weren't willing to pay an excessive premium. We tried to find the true value of the company. There was a lot of equipment, so we hired equipment appraisers. The company has real estate, so we hired real estate appraisers. Then we did the valuation of the goodwill, the intangibles: the cash flow, what we felt the market value was, and so on. We aggregated all that, and after several months of work—and a lot of money—we proposed the valuation to the first generation. They didn't like our numbers even though they were as real and objective as we could make them. They wanted a lot more money for the business than the group was willing to pay.

The situation got fraught and filled with risk. At stake were jobs, annual bonuses, and the need to all work together every day. The fabric of the family was being impacted because the generations weren't aligned. The founders always had the big carrot: "You guys are going to own this someday!" It seemed the founders never expected that the group would buy them out. Someday is always a ways away. We don't think they were prepared for the moment someday became today, which was why the transaction had challenges.

After two years of negotiations, we finally got everyone to agree to a value and structure. The second generation thinks it's too much, but this is a situation of affording a little bit too much. The cousins know that they're overpaying. They're not happy about it, but they know they can't gain control any other way. Even though they're getting paid a lot for the company, the founders still probably feel like they left too much money on the table. Both sides feel like they didn't get everything they wanted, but the deal still got done—that's the sign of a good deal.

WIDENING GAPS

When you find out that you're not aligned with the seller on a particular issue, especially if it's a major issue, it's as if you're on thin ice. You try to get off that piece of ice, but the quicker you run from it, the more it keeps cracking under you. If the issue is small, the gap between buyer and seller is small and can be bridged. But when you say, "Look, you're way off on that price," or "You're nuts if you think I'm getting out under those terms," that destabilizes everything. All the little cracks come out, and all around it the ice just shatters—and sometimes creates more gaps.

"I'm not paying you a nickel more than what I think it's worth!" "Oh, and by the way, you have environmental problems on the property!" "We can't get it financed." "We caught you lying." The gaps get bigger. All of a sudden, the things that didn't matter at all now matter a lot.

Widening gaps might sound like a bad thing, but often that's how we find a way to get out of the deal completely or get a better deal for our client. Gaps can frequently create opportunity.

FIND THE OPPORTUNITY

When the gaps surface, our job is to make sure we fill the gaps as quickly as we can. Buyers and sellers are seldom able to fix these things by themselves. Solutions are about pivoting: "This avenue doesn't work. What's the alternative?" We ask ourselves, "What are the most creative approaches we can take to fill this gap?"

Many times, we've thought the gap was so wide it was

insurmountable. Then, we'd get up the next morning and discover ways to bridge it. Perhaps we found an opportunity for the seller, or for the buyer—maybe even for both.

But that initial "Uh-oh, we've got a problem" can be fatal. We do our best to keep the pathway stable. We try not to panic when it's bad news or get overly excited when it's good news. It's like playing cards. If you get a great card, you don't jump for joy. If you get a bad one, you don't show your hand either.

Stay focused on the goal of doing what is best for the continued success of the company. Both buyers and sellers often lose sight of that. The transaction becomes personal, and people do or say things that cause damage. It's our job to keep the focus on the company, not the personalities.

The company is the golden goose. You can't expect it to keep laying eggs if everyone is treating it like a punching bag. People can get more invested in proving a point than in keeping the company going.

If both sides are ready to accept the new realities as they arise and negotiate in good faith, it's time to develop your strategy.

9

DEFINE STRATEGY

The foundation of any deal is trying to meet the goals of both the buyer and the seller. Each transaction, however, is weighted to one side. One side will always have the advantage.

We once worked with a seller who wanted to have an insider buy the company. He told us, "I want you to sell the company to this employee. She doesn't have much money at all, but she's the right person to carry on the firm. Make this work for me and for her."

We structured the deal so the advantages were on the seller's side. We made some efforts to balance things out fairly, but ultimately, if you were to ask who was the winner in the deal, it was the seller. The seller wanted to time the deal so that it maximized his ability to move the proceeds into his 401(k). It would have benefitted the buyer to do the sale earlier, but she didn't have any leverage in the situation. While it came down to what he wanted, the deal was still good for her, because she couldn't have bought the business any other way.

We've been working on the internal succession plan for another client for more than six years. He's already passed 45 percent of the company on to a distant cousin, a son-in-law, and a daughter, and he's phasing out. He wants to reward them because they've been vital to the growth of this very lucrative organization.

At first, his goals and their goals were aligned. As time went by, however, the goals of the second generation diverged. They want to invest in real estate, but the founder just wants to keep making money and live the lifestyle he's become accustomed to.

Both sides talk to us separately. The second generation thinks it's time for the founder to step aside and that we should facilitate that. The founder tells us he's not happy with being pushed out. Because he owns 55 percent of the company, neither side can afford to push the other one out. The second generation wants to expand, and without them, the founder doesn't have anyone to run the company.

We're trying to facilitate a deal that satisfies everyone,

which means the less they call us to complain, the happier our days go! It's our job to make sure the company is as healthy as possible. We represent all the individuals, but we really represent the company.

THE SELLER'S MIND

Sellers have countless motivations driving the decision to sell. Understanding those reasons is key to negotiating a successful transfer. As a buyer, you need to be careful of situations where the seller is being pushed to sell by outside pressures. If the seller is selling for reasons besides a basic desire to leave the business, you might find they give short shrift to the transaction. They're not selling on their own terms, and that can affect the deal by adding emotions to it.

IT ALL STARTS AT HOME

Family issues and estate issues are often very complicated drivers that guide the seller's mind throughout the transaction. They might talk about selling a lot, but they don't want to pull the trigger. As an example, they might have a spouse at home who wants to be doing other things with their life, rather than being beholden to the business. In these situations, the spouse is driving the deal forward more than the seller.

On occasion, we have clients who, for whatever reason,

don't want their kids to have the business. One client had a son who felt entitled to be in the business, even though he didn't want to do much in the way of actual hands-on work to learn the business. Mom and Dad had decidedly different opinions on his continued presence in the business, which prevented the situation from being corrected.

Eventually, the family spun off a division to give the son a place to go and establish himself. That business eventually failed due to his inability to manage the business and accept advice and guidance. He is back in the family business in a lesser role, never to be the successor that he envisioned. It's still a point of contention for Mom and Dad.

One of our clients had a history of family succession. Three generations had worked their way up from the shop floor to the role of CEO. Like his father and grandfather before him, our client brought in his son, who also worked his way up. When he decided to sell, he sold to an outsider. He only told his son the business wouldn't be his right before the sale went through. The decision was devastating to his son—a huge disappointment. We were very disappointed by his decision and tried to talk him out of it but were unsuccessful in doing so.

We had another client who felt his son would be happier if he were out of the family business but didn't know how to have that conversation. We weren't able to help—sometimes family matters are beyond our influence.

As a buyer, it can be difficult to understand the seller's family dynamics, but it's your job to learn them. An internal buyer may already have some handle on the situation. You have to think about those dynamics and understand what's going on behind the scenes before you make the final decision to move forward.

Estates are a different situation. When an owner has passed away, sometimes you can get a better deal as a buyer, because no one in the estate has the ability or interest to run the company. On the other hand, you may not have as much flexibility in structuring the deal. You also may have to deal with a lot of emotions on the sell side, especially if you're buying as an insider. The family may feel the business is worth much more than it really is, while you are willing to pay only what the business owes the bank, leaving the family with a lot less. You may have to deal with a lot of bitterness from the family after the deal is done.

KNOW THEIR POSITION

You want to know where the other side is coming from in the long and short term, as well as in the present moment. What do they need to feel satisfied with the transaction?

Usually, we're talking about financial needs but not always. The seller might want to take more time off, to focus on hobbies or travel. Other times, sellers are focused on making sure family members are taken care of in the transaction. You can have a situation where the seller wants to make sure that Uncle Jimmy, who has some health issues, always has a job with the new owners. We have a client who's put everyone on payroll because his dad gave him a legacy list that includes taking care of his brother and sister as part of the buyout. It's like parents who keep paying their kid's cell phone bill. Let's just say, we have a lot of cell phones promised.

DON'T SHOW YOUR HAND

Sellers tend to be talkative. They'll tell you exactly what they need.

Once you discover the needs of a seller, you have to play your cards right. Don't panic. Whatever the seller needs, there are ways to get there. Now's the time to listen, not talk. Don't react to anything. Just listen, thank the seller, and say you'll get back to them.

When you do, come back to them with a well-rounded and well-defined response, not just a declaration of "We're not paying you that." As advisors, we coach that response. Don't get overly excited one way or the other.

Aggressive body language, curt remarks—those can blow a deal forever. Sellers have long memories; buyers need to have short ones. As a buyer, always keep the end goal in mind.

THE ART OF STRATEGY

With buyers, we spend a lot of time helping them figure out the transaction's equation, finding the point where it's time to move ahead or cut your losses. If we know a buyer can't afford the asking price or will have trouble getting the financing, we need to identify those questions before they come up at a meeting.

THE PARTNER BUYOUT

We had a situation where we had a buyer and a seller who were partners. One, who's been active in the business, was going to buy out the other, who's been inactive. He's tired of paying him $300,000 a year. The inactive partner's leverage is the business has heavy debt, and it's secured by the inactive partner's guarantee and assets.

When we structured the deal, we had to find a way to balance these pieces. The inactive partner wanted to get his money out, because he was off to do something else. We had to structure the transaction in a manner that gave the buyer flexibility to make regular payments and paid a premium to the seller—and also took the premium back if the buyer was able to find a way to buy the seller out for a lump sum.

The deal had many moving parts, including stockholder loans. We ended up structuring a monthly guarantee fee for every month that the inactive partner is still on as a personal guarantor. It's enough for him to feel like he's getting something for the risk of carrying the debt. And it's enough to motivate the active partner to do everything he can to get the other one off the hook.

This buyout required a lot of strategy and a deal structure that met each one of the respective partners' requirements. Even though he was inactive in the business, the seller felt entitled to a lot. After all, he did own 50 percent of the company.

We're in the process of dealing with another, similar transaction. The inactive partner's goal seems to be to inflict pain on the other partner. Unfortunately, you never know where a partnership will take you. It's like getting married—you start out with high hopes.

STRATEGY STARTS WITH PREPARATION

When you're doing a deal, think like a Boy Scout: "Be prepared." You need to understand where you can and cannot push. Everyone knows their breaking point. In one deal, everything nearly collapsed over a $400-a-month car payment for the seller's sister.

If you know where you can push on the seller, you know where you can win. At that point, the seller wasn't going to push on a $400-a-month item and potentially lose his whole deal. You have to know when to concede on a minor point.

SHIFTING PRIORITIES

What's important at the start of the negotiation may not be important toward the end, and vice versa. Things may take on heightened importance in the negotiations, because they're leverage points. That car payment suddenly became very important. It doesn't necessarily matter why. It's not always rational, but you have to deal with the individual's stubbornness and psychology. In some cases, you may see someone throw these things out there as smokescreens, because there's something else they want. Suddenly, something that was out there as a minor part becomes a very big issue, because now someone else wants something that they weren't getting.

The buyer always has to figure out what's important to the seller, but those things can shift during the deal. You can get trapped by changing demands if you're not careful.

As a buyer, you must realize that a seller's shifting needs and motivations often go beyond money. Or that's what the buyer says. When someone tells us, "It's not about the money," or "I just want everyone to be happy," or "I only want my company to succeed," we keep negotiating. We find out it's almost always about the money in the end. Listen to what the seller says, but be wary.

Now that you know how to hone your strategy, it's time to work on the transaction mechanics.

10

TRANSACTION MECHANICS

What are transaction mechanics? Let's walk through the process. When we have a buyer, we start with some initial conversations with the buyer and the seller so that we have some parameters of what each side is thinking. Both parties probably already agree about some likely general numbers or general terms.

From there, we create a Letter of Intent (LOI), which is a nonbinding document outlining what the parties have agreed to. We negotiate the key points of the deal from that standpoint.

Once that LOI gets signed, you bring in your attorneys and the bank financing starts. We start to develop the asset purchase agreements or the stock purchase agreements, you do your due diligence, and negotiations continue to get to the closing point. Then, once you close, you sign all the documents and own the company.

The components of a deal all work together like a machine, and if they're not working perfectly together, the deal can break down quickly. If a buyer doesn't understand the steps and processes, he gets very frustrated. Generally, the seller understands the process much better than the buyer. The seller has already got the business on the market and made decisions on pricing and terms. The buyer has the steepest learning curve, because he has to catch up with the seller.

Understanding all this is expensive and time-consuming. Buyers get angry much more often than sellers. Waiting on all the steps can be painful. If you're working with a bank for financing, you've got to wait on appraisals. You might have to wait on real estate inspections. You might have to wait while the documents are drafted and the commitment letter is written. There's a lot of moving parts and you need to be patient and wait for them all to come to completion.

DETAILS, DETAILS

As advisors, we try to drive the steps forward and educate both sides. But we can't perform all the due diligence ourselves. We can tell you what information and documents to request, and we can give our perspectives on them, but ultimately, the buyer has to decide the right questions to ask. The seller has to decide if they're comfortable with the buyer. You must be willing to pay for the time and energy it takes to figure these things out.

The LOI and the purchase and seller agreement have a lot of details, but often, neither side has the patience for them. We do, and a lot of mistakes can be avoided by good advisors who can coach you through your impatience. They can keep you on track. We're good at that—check our website at www.acg.org for more information on how we can help.

Sometimes people try to negotiate the LOI too much, and it gets bogged down. Sometimes the buyer may be too aggressive and try to negotiate too much too soon. They may want to know everything right now, when a lot of times it's better to figure things out as we go, because the little things up front can become deal killers in the beginning. If they come up when you're further into the transaction, they just become details to negotiate. The deeper you get into things, the harder it is to walk away. That's a calculated risk sometimes. No one wants to spend money and then lose a deal because they didn't have a deal point negotiated successfully.

EVERY DEAL HAS THE SAME STEPS

Let's talk about each step of the deal in detail.

THE LETTER OF INTENT

The deal starts with each party signing the LOI. The LOI includes the names of the parties and who is a party to the agreement, or who may be a party to the agreement at a later date. Usually, the Letter of Intent allows the parties to be nominees or assignees of the agreement.

What's Being Purchased

The LOI usually then defines what's being purchased. You might be purchasing specific assets, such as the furniture, fixtures, and equipment (FF&E) and goodwill. Are you purchasing inventory, or are you not? Is it a stock transaction or an asset transaction?

With an asset transaction, you're purchasing both the physical assets and then the intangible assets of the company. There's a price assigned to those. If you're purchasing the stock, then what's included in that company at closing?

Also, is cash included or excluded? Is the working capital included or excluded? Are there certain liabilities that aren't going to be assumed? Are there going to be items that are going to be excluded, such as a personal vehicle or personal property?

The Structure of Payment

Once we've identified what we're buying, then it's time to structure the payment. For instance, the LOI would state what amount's going to be in cash and what will be in the seller's notes. If it's an asset purchase, the allocation of the price is specified, with the amounts allocated to goodwill, fixed assets, and so on stated.

Contingencies

From there, the offer is typically contingent upon the "following terms and conditions." You usually see some very basic things such as "Contingent on all assets being sold free and clear of all claims and liabilities." Financing contingencies are also included, such as "Contingent on financing to the buyer's satisfaction." Employment agreements, consulting agreements, noncompete agreements, and the like are included here.

Leases are also included in contingencies. You may see language regarding who's responsible for whose fees in this section, along with requirements for inspections. The due diligence period is laid out there, including when it starts and how it's done.

If it's a stock deal, typically more terms and conditions regarding the types of representations and warranties are in this section. So is language regarding the type of accounting principles that will be used. There might be formulas related to the calculation of EBITDA. You may then have language regarding what happens in the event of disputes, such as where it gets resolved and what state law is in place.

Exclusivity and Deposits

The LOI typically contains a set period of time for exclusivity. There may be language requiring notification if any other offers are received. If there's a good faith deposit, it's in this section. You may see some language that lets you walk away if there's material adverse changes to the business.

The definitive date through which the LOI is valid is here. When the purchase is going to be executed and when the closing date will be set are in this section.

Nonbinding Language

A LOI typically has language that confirms it's nonbinding.

Having a LOI is great, but at the end of the day, you don't have to actually do what you said you were going to do.

The LOI simply lays out the terms so that negotiations can begin. It's a road map. It serves as a framework, identifying the key parties and points. The transaction doesn't become binding until you have a purchase agreement order or a stock purchase agreement. What that LOI does do, once both parties sign off on it, is trigger all exclusivity and the deposit.

Now you start your process.

THE PURCHASE AGREEMENT

The Purchase Agreement is the next step. This is the definitive document for the transfer of the business and it is legally binding. Getting it right is crucial for a successful transition. The process can take a while, but patience will be rewarded.

Accountants

Your accountants should enter the picture early on to look at the tax ramifications of the deal for each side. The seller should certainly have talked to his accountant before things progressed this far. Because so much of the acquisitions today are goodwill, taxes have a substantial impact on the profitability of the company and the cash flow. Typically, the seller likes goodwill because of the capital gains tax rate on selling it. It's very advantageous for them, as opposed to the rate for other assets.

Seek out an accountant with transactional experience, so they can review documents and make comments, especially on the financing side. Your accountant can examine and evaluate the preliminary projections. Your accountant can also help analyze the tax write-offs for goodwill. Under IRS Code Section 197, goodwill is an intangible asset that can take fifteen years to be completely written off. It's a very slow process. Chances are, you'll have the business paid for and you'll still be writing off the intangibles. If you buy equipment, you might be able to write it off in one year, under special code sections. If you buy a vehicle, it might be five years. Everything has a different depreciable life to it.

Make sure to pick a firm that has experience in structuring deals and that understands tax consequences. Your accounting firm is also likely doing your projections. That means you need an accounting firm that understands the industry you're buying into and can apply common sense and experience to the numbers. A good accountant on each side should be able to communicate and find common ground for the buyer and the seller, because there's no such thing as everyone getting the entire win.

Attorneys

In a stock deal, the buyer's attorney typically drafts the stock sale agreement and the seller's attorney drafts the asset sale. If it's a simple deal—maybe just a bill of sale and nothing much else—an attorney can draft for both sides. With that said, we always try to have our client's counsel draft the document. It's advantageous to use your document and language, because it's written from your point of view. Your attorneys will help you understand what type of agreements are on the table, the amounts under discussion, and what's negotiable and what isn't.

The bank's attorneys enter after the agreement is signed and the due diligence starts. Banks have long since stopped closing on deals without legal counsel for themselves, because they had so many problems with defaults and reneging on terms and conditions. The bank has its own lawyers, but the buyer has to pay for them, which is always very contentious. Buyers pay for bank counsel. Banks pay for nothing.

The bank does tell you which law firm they're going to hire. We try to get a price range on the fees, so our buyer knows what to expect. You can also expect to pay for appraisals and valuations if any are required.

Develop a Deal over Time

It's hard to keep an opinion from fronting a deal, but you don't want to get dragged down into unimportant squabbles. We once scheduled a closing on a July 3. It should have been very quick. The closing started at 10:00 a.m. and we didn't get out of there till eleven o'clock at night. What held it up were things that should never have come into play, unimportant details. They didn't matter much to either party until they suddenly mattered to the other party. Those little issues cost the buyer several thousand dollars.

You don't want to get bogged down by nuances that often-times aren't important. People fight over the wrong things. This can be a manifestation of their psychological inability to let go: "I don't want to let go. I don't want to give up control." It's definitely about control. The stress of selling a business can overwhelm your perspective.

Due Diligence

Due diligence is the comprehensive assessment of all aspects of the business by the buyer. Due diligence can cover anything you can and cannot imagine. We have some due diligence checklists that are fourteen, fifteen, twenty pages long—single spaced. If you're buying a business, obviously there's financial due diligence. Then there's operational due diligence, due diligence on sales, due diligence on human resources, due diligence on technology, and due diligence on environmental issues. And all those areas have a lot of different subcategories. For example, if it's due diligence for human resources, that may include reviewing the employee handbook, vacation policy, sick days policy, and going through employment files.

Due diligence requires someone to do some real work. A lot of our clients think due diligence means just asking questions, but you need to dig in. To take the HR example, you need to know all the details, down to when the lunch hours are and the nonsmoking policy on the property. Are the personnel files up to date? HR is a huge issue today because of the risk exposure to an employer.

Issues can fly under the radar during due diligence. We worked with a client who bought a company that had a fleet of vehicles. You know what he didn't do? Get the vehicles checked out. After he closed, he realized that these vehicles were breaking down constantly. The company was spending tons of money in maintenance. It was a problem hiding in plain sight. They ended up having to spend a quarter of a million dollars on new vehicles. If they were paying attention, they would have said, "Let's get a mechanic to look at the vehicles."

Due diligence can get complicated. If the buyer doesn't have the expertise to do all of it themselves, we recommend outsourcing it to an expert. We bring people in all the time for that. We love due diligence from the buying side. We hate it on the selling side.

Sellers hate due diligence because it shows them in their underwear. In due diligence, you look at everything, from top to bottom. You're looking for bad things to do either one of two things: convince yourself not to buy into the deal, or get a lower price.

Due diligence can often turn up something that blows up the deal, or at least makes you renegotiate the price. "You didn't tell us that there were only three major customers. You said there were ten major customers!" That's a big thing, but even little things can add up and blow away the deal.

When we're representing sellers during due diligence, we're constantly cautioning them not to get angry, not to blow up, and not to lose their cool, because it's the job of the buyer to find the problems. If problems do come up, the buyer can leverage the situation. You need to figure out which aspects of your discoveries to play up and which ones to let slide. You have to be organized and intelligent about it, and you can't be accusatory. When you find things, you've got to be well-prepared, but don't get crazy over them. You might have ten due diligence questions. One of them may be important and the other nine may not. Be careful how you play it out with the seller, because the seller can also say, "Get the hell out of here. I'm done with you. You're driving me nuts asking me stupid questions." If you're not careful, the deal can blow up during due diligence.

Numbers Don't Lie

Be prepared for the numbers. Know how to use the surprises.

You can't buy a business unless the numbers make sense. There are all sorts of variables. You must be prepared to get your projections done and your financing done and see what the risk and reward is based on what's in front of you. What you uncovered during due diligence is extremely important. Be prepared for the numbers. They can create a buyer's advantage. It's our favorite part.

Let's say you have a great relationship with the seller, and everything's going along great, and all of a sudden, you, the buyer, notice something in the numbers that doesn't make sense to you. If you're smart, you're going to go to the seller and you're going to act hurt, you're going to be wounded, you're going to be saddened that something just doesn't look right here, Mr. Seller. "You had told me X, and now I've found out Y, and I'm depressed, I'm anxious over it, and I don't know whether I can go on."

And now the seller has to become very defensive and try to figure it out. If you hold your mark, you're probably going to get a reduced price, or you're going to get better terms. That's the only way the seller can make you comfortable, when you've got your long face on and you look like you're going to cry.

We've been doing this for more than forty years; we can guarantee you the seller will change the terms or reduce the price a little bit, or help you through this particular issue in some other manner. Let's say you're looking at customer receivables and you ask the seller, "How long does it take to collect?" "Usually forty-five to sixty days," he replies. Then you're doing your due diligence and see two or three of his major customers are 90 days or 120 days past due. Well, that changes the whole picture. You say, "Now I don't have the cash flow to pay you your payments." He replies, "Well, don't make payments for the first 120 days."

There are always advantages you can use, if you're not annoying and obnoxious about it. If you put the seller on a hard defense right away, there will be pushback. If you put him on the defensive in a soft manner, you're going to get ahead. You're going to be able to carve him up a little bit. You say, "I bring this up more in sorrow than in anger." You bring it up that you're wounded when you have your carving knife out.

In some cases, if the seller can justify that your due diligence findings are incorrect or not something to be concerned about, if a good seller is prepared for that, the buyer can be convinced that it's OK. In most cases, though, if you found something odd in due diligence, it's not OK. It's not something that can be explained away.

If you have a chance to go through contracts or you get to talk to employees, you may find during your due diligence that your seller has been pricing a particular product or service wrongly. He's not making the margins on the jobs he should be, and you've relied on false information to prepare your projections. You can certainly corner a seller with that.

A smart seller should disclose customer concentration from one customer up front. He should say, "I've got a hundred customers, but one of them is 35 percent of my business." When we're representing sellers, we are very open about concentration in the offering memorandum. But sometimes sellers don't disclose this information.

If you don't already know about concentration from just one customer and it comes up in the due diligence, it can be a key negotiating point. We bought an aerospace company many years ago that had GE as its only customer. They were doing a good volume, but it drove the value into the ground because of the concern that the customer can be gone tomorrow.

Taxes

What does the buyer need to know about taxes besides they are expensive and that the tax laws are ever changing?

Taxes should come to light early. So far, we've talked a

lot about the allocations, which is important. Obviously, what's good for the buyer is not good for the seller. That's very true. And we've talked about how two accountants should find the best resolution. When you're doing your projections for the bank and for yourself, it's critical to understand what the tax cost is going be. Taxes shouldn't be confused with cash flow issues. Taxes are paid on profit. That converts to a cash flow issue.

It's imperative to have a good accountant who understands the deal's effective tax rate. It's not just allocations; it's also "What's it going to cost me as I own this company? Am I going to have enough profit coming out after tax?" Tax planning is critical. When the tax on a company is in the 40 to 50 percent bracket between state and federal, that can take a lot of the glitter off the deal.

If the projections aren't good, the deal will blow up in someone's face fast. Bad projections are almost criminal—not that we haven't been involved in them on both sides. Our stomachs get tight when we have to do projections for someone. We never let projections out in our firm without two or three senior people taking another look at them and asking us to justify how we got there. They want to see notes and assumptions. "How did you assume you were going to get that level of sales? What are you using for inflation periods?" "Do you know something that's going to make those sales move up or down?"

Unfortunately, there are some accountants who say to the client, "What would you like the projection to be?" or "How would you like these to look for the bank?" And then they find a way to get there. That's a disaster waiting to happen, especially for the accountant. They could easily be sued.

Legal Issues

How you structure the company depends on how the deal works out. Every state has some variance in company structure. Lots of people form their companies in Delaware, because it's a very friendly and inexpensive state for business. If you're in high-cost states such as New York, Massachusetts, Connecticut, Rhode Island, and New Jersey, forming a corporation is usually very expensive, plus you have pricey annual renewal fees.

Because of our tax background, we want to put together a corporate structure that has some flexibility for our buyer, our buyer's family, and our buyer's long-term plans. We may have a buyer who says, "I can't afford a retirement plan the first year, and I can't afford health insurance, and maybe I can't get a corporate car yet, but we want a structure there where we're going to be able to get that later."

We also address lifestyle issues. We sit down with our buyers and say, "What are all the things in life that you need?" "Well, I want to put my wife on the payroll, and I have a fifteen-year-old son who's going to be going to college soon." You go through that list and figure out if an LLC or a Subchapter S corporation or a C corporation, or some other business structure is best to meet those goals. Those structures are important to your future earnings, but they're also important to the deal structure.

They're also important for asset protection. If a husband and wife are buying a business, maybe only one of the spouses should own the business, because there's risk with the business. Maybe the spouse who doesn't have the risk should own the house. Asset protection also comes into play for structuring for a buyer on the legal side.

At some point down the line, you can change the corporate structure if it becomes necessary. It can be painful, however, because of the tax ramifications on the transfer of assets. Your accountant and lawyer are important here to help you see the long-run picture. When might the company get sold? Are you going to have to liquidate? Will you outgrow a particular entity? When you do replacements, what's the tax cost? You do need to look down the road a little bit.

If you're planning to pass the company down to the next generation, you might use an S corporation. LLCs work very well, because you can bring new partners in. They can own some capital, but they don't have to get any of the income. We use them a lot when we have parents who own assets, maybe businesses or real estate, and have children who are part of the succession plan. The LLC will allow Mom and Dad to continue receiving income on an annual basis without having to give that up, but the kids start to acquire some capital. We use it a lot for real estate and estate planning and elder care planning.

TRANSACTION TIMING

The typical time frame from LOI to the closing of the deal is sixty to ninety days. You need to be careful the deal doesn't go stale. If you're a buyer and you're dragging it out too long and torturing the poor seller, or if you're a seller torturing the buyer by not giving him enough time for due diligence, you're going to run out of goodwill. Be careful how you drag things out. We see people go dark on us, and the minute that happens, we know the deal's in trouble. People get distracted, they get cold feet, they found another deal, their stomach muscles tighten. There are a lot of reasons for a deal to drag on without closing.

In the purchase and sell agreement, the language might indicate time is of the essence. The agreement specifies the time frame for closing. If you're the buyer, you're in real trouble if you sign that agreement and you don't understand what those five words mean. They mean you have to close within the specified time. If you don't, your deposit is at risk, and you may get sued for not doing the deal timely or at all.

If you can, strike that language or don't sign it unless you're absolutely confident that you can perform in that time. Of course, sellers seldom agree if you want to strike it. Their lawyers put it in there because you've got a closing coming. But good lawyers know that you can only push that so far.

Stay Calm

We talk a lot about the numbers and due diligence, but we also know that buyers will rely on instinct along with the facts. That's fine, as long as you're also moving forward with good advisors who can tell you when your instincts are mistaken or your emotions are getting in the way of reality.

Stay calm. There's no reason to anger anyone, unless the negotiation really gets bad. In that case, you're better off letting your advisors take that heat. Burning bridges in deals is not good. Let your advisors push and shove for you. That's part of their job. The calmer you stay, the better you look as a buyer.

That doesn't mean you can't be firm, and it doesn't mean

there can't be a time when you should sit down with the seller and say, "Look, I'm being firm for the following reasons..." But that doesn't mean you need to start calling the seller names. Don't punch anyone.

Don't assume anything, not even goodwill. Don't even assume good intentions on the seller's part. Have a blank slate. You don't have to be cynical, and you don't have to be nasty about it.

We're ready to move forward. Your team is in place. Everybody's in your corner. Everybody understands what's going on, and it's time to finance the deal.

PART III

CLOSE

11

FINANCE THE DEAL

In most small and mid-size transactions, seller financing is a reality of the deal. This is true whether it's an inside deal or an outside deal. We once represented a buyer who was purchasing a similar business as an add-on to his own but in a different geographic area. The idea was that it was a similar business in another market that had some synergies with the one he already owned.

He found a seller who had been on the market for a long time. It seemed like a good fit, and we put in a lot of time on the due diligence. The seller was very interested in financing part of the deal. He made a lot of promises and statements during the courting period suggesting that he was all in for whatever was necessary on the financing. He claimed he didn't care about what he got from the closing; he just needed to know the company was going to be sold and would provide him an annuity for his retirement.

When we looked at the business, we realized it was highly leveraged and the financing was going to be a little tough. A couple of local banks were interested, but they wouldn't come on board without a lot of seller financing. Our client didn't have a lot of money to put down to buy the new business, but the one he owned was operating well. We put together a LOI, which was accepted by both parties. The LOI had the transaction contingent upon seller financing.

As we got closer to executing the purchase and sale, the broker on the other side contacted us and said that the seller wasn't as interested in financing as much of the deal as he had hoped. He would still finance some, but there were going to be some new rules of the road. He wanted to stay at the company two or three years to bridge the gap before he turned sixty-six, and he wanted his son to stay on the payroll. He wanted to guarantee that his son would have an employment contract with an escape clause and that his spouse would stay on the payroll for six months. He also wanted a truck available to him, in exchange for financing the portion of the price he had committed to.

The broker on the other side was, obviously, very concerned, because his client had already executed a LOI. While the LOI was nonbinding legally, the parties had worked through it and executed it. We had spent a lot of time and money based on the belief that the deal would be financed by the seller, and now he was backing away.

Our buyer, who wasn't a particularly patient individual, started to push back. He decided the interest rate was too high, and he didn't like the other requirements either. The seller had him hooked—he had the bait of financing. Our client took the bait, and was going to pay, even though it was a thin deal. But as the seller got greedier and more concerned with his contingencies, he lost the bait and our client swam away. Eventually, the deal completely fell apart over the financing.

SELLER FINANCING

We always expect challenges with seller financing for an outside transaction, because the parties don't know each other. Inside transactions can be even more challenging, because the parties do know each other. It's not uncommon for the buyer and seller to make unrealistic assumptions about the other's situation.

In one internal buyout we did, our client was a highly compensated employee and the chosen successor. From the start of discussions, we made it clear that the buyer didn't have much money to put into the deal. The seller still proposed a deal that expected our client to come up with a big cash payment. Because the buyer was paid a lot of money, the seller somehow thought he managed to sock away several hundred thousand dollars while working for him. It wasn't a rational assumption. The seller's attitude about the buyer and the deal changed. He became worried that the buyer wasn't fiscally responsible and not capable of running the company. The deal died. With this deal, as with many others, there was a lot of love in the room before the realities of financing hit. Then it went away.

One of the challenges of seller financing in an internal transaction is that the seller is conflicted. On the one hand, they want to sell to the insider because they want them to have the business. At the same time, because the business is probably the largest source of wealth for the seller, they want to protect that wealth as much as possible.

When structuring seller financing in a deal, we try to strike a balance between the needs of the parties. If at all possible, we try to have our buyers provide some money up front. It doesn't have to be a lot but enough to show a commitment to the transaction. We also like to secure some funds from a third party, such as a bank, if at all possible. We like to see the seller financing structured with favorable terms. We might suggest a longer amortization period with a balloon payment, or interest-only payments for a period of time, or quarterly or annual payments instead of monthly payments, or scaling interest rates.

In conjunction with these options, we also like to consider the addition of a seller's premium. This might be a higher purchase price incorporated into financing, or the use of an earnout, or alternative compensation in the form of perquisites such as continuation of insurance, vehicle reimbursement, excess rent, and so on.

The use of alternative compensation can be particularly useful for a buyer. These costs can be taken as an expense, thereby reducing the taxable income for a buyer. This is particularly useful when the buyer is acquiring the stock of the company, which doesn't provide the benefit of depreciation and amortization.

As a buyer, you'll generally be loath to pay any more than you have to, so the idea of paying perquisites will be frustrating. The point to remember is that with a leveraged buyout, you are essentially buying them out with their own money. As time goes on and the business grows, the pain of those payments diminishes.

FINANCING OPTIONS: THE THREE FS

The first piece of the capital structure of the deal is putting some of your own money into the mix. If you don't have two nickels to rub together, you have three options to consider for this component.

FRIENDS AND FAMILY

Friends and family want to see you succeed and want

to be a part of that success. They're a logical source of capital when buying a business. They not only want to help, but they frequently want to make money as well. Investing in you is an opportunity to benefit from your potential success.

If someone you know well and love comes to you and says, "Hey, I need some help. I need a few grand to get me through a tough time, or I'm going to expand, or I'm going to buy a little business," you're inclined to open that checkbook because of your faith in them as a friend or family member. These people are the hardest to ask for money. When they give it, frequently they give it without thinking things through and understanding the likelihood of seeing that money ever again.

Taking money from them can be a bad decision. In most cases, family and friends are not sophisticated investors who understand the risk of giving you money. If you give someone $5,000 to go into the accounting business, you're probably going to get your money back, but that might not be the case with riskier business transactions. Banks and smart investors don't want to touch speculative enterprises—bars, restaurants, and sports events, for example—with a ten-foot pole. It comes down to family and friends. If there aren't a lot of strings attached, and if people understand the risk, family and friends are a great resource for more speculative endeavors.

If you get friends and family to invest in you, you have to be able to handle a lot of pressure, particularly if it's a significant investment for that person. We encourage you not to take money from family unless it's in the form of a gift or you're certain they understand that they may not get the money back. An investor should never risk more than they can afford to lose. It's a good rule of thumb to apply to the discussion you have with them.

If you do decide to take family or friend money and it's with the expectation of a return in a certain period of time, be prepared for the relationship between you and that person to change. If the business is slow or runs into trouble and you can't live up to the terms, be prepared to suffer. There's nothing worse than going to Christmas Eve dinner with your family when you haven't paid them back.

Another key piece to communicate to a family or friend member is that they are an investor, not the owner responsible for operating the business. A lot of parents want to help their kids get started in life and will help with the financing if you come to them with what seems like a reasonable business proposition. If family money comes without a lot of strings attached, it can be a huge help. It needs to be made clear that their investment doesn't allow them to give unsolicited advice. Family and friends who help with financing tend to forget that.

The bottom line is, if you are going to take money from family and friends, be clear up front about the risk, the expectations, and the realities of the situation. Communicate this constantly throughout the investment process and afterward. And put it all down in writing.

FOOLS

A fool is a person who may be eager to work with a buyer looking for help—they love the idea of being part of a deal. We've seen a lot of these. The fool puts money into a deal even though he has no idea what type of deal it is, what's going on, or what any of the financials are. He just wants to put some money in the deal because he thinks it's a good investment. He usually thinks it's a winner because he knows the buyer personally. He thinks, "I can't make anything just leaving the money in the bank, so I ought to give this guy five grand to buy into his bar because I know he sells a lot of booze and he's successful." This is a very, very, very common fool. And a very careless one. This approach is like buying stock on a hot tip or betting the house on a racehorse.

Fools can be great because they give you money without asking questions. The problem is, they turn bad when they don't get their money out. They can be worse than other investors. They can be your worst nightmare. If your neighbor gives you $5,000 to buy into a deal and then, in six months, you have to tell your neighbor to come over so that you can let him know his money is gone, guess what? You're not a good neighbor anymore and things can get really awkward.

Some fools will give you money because of who you are. In fact, we've been fools a few times in our careers. Fools have a lot of faith you, they believe in you, and they want to help you get started. Being a fool can provide a lot of emotional satisfaction. We've helped a lot of young people get into a business. Has it paid off? We've never kept score, because we'd go nuts. It's like going to bat. You can't bat a thousand, but you might get a single—or you might strike out. We've never loaned money or invested money with anyone and made a windfall. It's never happened, and we've been around a long time. The bottom line: if you are going to take money from a fool be prepared for a bad situation and protect yourself accordingly. Have the same conversation you have with your family and friends and get everything in writing.

DEBT FINANCING

Most of our clients consider conventional lenders before they turn to sources such as the internet. There are different sources for this type of financing.

BANKS

If the deal is good, the banks are there. They price according to the risk, and their interest rates are usually very good. Everyone always assumes that banks will finance everything, but it's important to remember that banks are very heavily regulated and conservative in nature. They wrap you up in covenants and take your firstborn and any piece of collateral they can attach themselves to. We always remind our buyers that the banks aren't investors; they're lenders. Lenders look at deals differently than investors do. They're focused on getting their money paid back, because otherwise, the regulators will shut them down.

SMALL BUSINESS ADMINISTRATION

When you start talking to a bank, you'll likely hear about the Small Business Administration (SBA), an independent agency of the federal government. The SBA doesn't loan money. What they do instead is guarantee the debt for the bank. If you want to purchase a business and you need money, and the bank says they like a deal but they think it's kind of risky, they'll bring in the SBA. The SBA will take a piece of that loan as part of the risk and guarantee it for the bank. The piece could be 50 percent or even up to 75 percent. The guarantee allows the bank some flexibility. They can still build a relationship with the client by providing the money, but they know if something blows up, they have a guarantee for part of that shortfall.

Today, there's a lot of shortfalls because hard asset acquisitions are less and less frequent. There's simply fewer and fewer businesses with tangible property such as machinery or vehicles. Now, a lot of the value is based on cash flow and goodwill and other intangibles. The lenders typically need an edge. They need someone to push them to make the deal. Enter the SBA or one of several other local guarantee groups. There are all sorts of funds and grant money. Even the Department of Agriculture has a lending program. The lenders, whether a conventional lender or a nonconventional lender, can reach out to many different government programs, right down to local agencies.

In your area, there might be community development grants, or maybe the municipality is giving tax breaks to a new buyer. They might offer tax credits, bond financing, or industrial revenue bonds that the banks will help secure. These are the more conservative options available to buyers.

When you go to the bank for a loan, they're going to evaluate your credit and what you have for cash and collateral. They'll also evaluate the seller's participation. Then they'll see what type of SBA guarantee they can give you. The SBA's maximum exposure amount is $3.75 million. So if you get an SBA-guaranteed loan for $5 million, the maximum guarantee to the lender will be $3.75 million, or 75 percent. The SBA has loans ear-marked for minorities and women-owned businesses. You have to be a US citizen.

To secure an SBA guarantee, your business plan must be accepted by the bank first. Then the bank takes it to the SBA. Some SBA loans can be approved in three to five days, but most others take much longer. Fees can be expensive and you can expect to spend some money on appraisals, but if it gets you to the bank, they can be considered the cost of doing business. If you're seeking financing, you've got to be prepared to pay these compliance costs.

The banks have to reserve less for loan losses when they've got an SBA guarantee. If a loan goes bad and they have a 50 percent guarantee from the SBA, they have to reserve for loan loss of only 50 percent. It's a huge advantage. If the bank wants to push you in that direction, you may or may not have a lot of choice, but it's not a bad way to go at all.

NONPROFITS

Many communities have nonprofit lenders that are established to provide capital and resources to underserved or higher risk segments. These groups are typically funded by the banks and are targeted at smaller transactions that a bank deems too risky to finance—think restaurants and personal service businesses. The banks are incentivized to fund these groups because they have Community Reinvestment Act (CRA) requirements.

The banks like it because they can outsource the risk, and

the loans are effective. The nonprofit is committed to your success and will frequently provide technical assistance to ensure the businesses they fund survive. They may get a better interest rate for it. They're getting more and more sophisticated all the time, which means they're getting smarter and better at making sure the companies they fund are successful.

UNDERSTANDING THE DRIVERS

Banks must be very, very certain about any loan they make. As a banker once explained to a group we were doing a Q&A with, if a bank delinquency rate is more than 1.5 percent, they're in trouble with regulators and stockholders. That means they need to be right 99 percent of the time, because otherwise, they're losing a lot of money. There aren't too many businesses where your success is contingent on always being right.

When the bank looks at your deal, they're looking at it from a risk profile. How much money do you have? How much of it is at risk with what the seller's doing? What do you have for collateral? What is the "air ball" between the collateral and the amount of the loan?

Banks take the expected cash flow of the business into consideration. They want to see a demonstrated track record that indicates the business can consistently pay the debt service at a certain level and meet the covenants that they'll offer. Typically, you see a 1.25 to 1 debt service coverage ratio, which means for every dollar in debt, you need to have $1.25 in cash flow.

Banks will also consider the guarantees, or the strength of the buyer. What are his guarantees worth? Does he own a home? Does he have any stocks and bonds? Does he have retirement accounts? His guarantee helps mitigate some of the risk. If you have a strong buyer with a good credit score who has proved himself worthy of being a borrower, that guarantee can reduce the interest rate. It certainly makes the bank more comfortable. If you have a guarantor with a bad credit score, he's probably not going to be able to buy the business.

Most of our transactions have seller financing in part because the bank wants to see seller financing as part of the equation. It mitigates their risk, but it also demonstrates that the seller has confidence in the business. If the seller doesn't want to participate in the financing, why should the bank?

INTERNET FINANCING

Securing bank financing can be really challenging. This has led to the rise of alternative lenders. A lot of companies have popped up on the internet that have investor money that they will loan under far more flexible terms and with a faster turnaround time. The interest rates are higher, but you're getting access to money very quickly.

Some sites are investment-oriented, and then there's crowdfunding sites such as Kickstarter and GoFundMe. For our clients, we think of internet funders such as Fundations and Next Up Capital that often solicit clients via mail. We've had several clients who have used them.

These companies definitely serve a purpose and have a place in the market today. They help an underserved part of the market. Let's say you wanted to borrow $25,000 or $30,000 for a very small business or startup, for working capital, or to grow your business, you go to the bank. You don't have a lot of collateral. Your credit score is good, but it's not quite good enough to take a personal loan. You go to one of these unconventional internet lenders, and you're likely going to have your $25,000, $50,000, or more within four or five days, if you have a decent credit score.

Their terms are usually good. They have substantially higher interest rates because they're in a risky business. The repayment terms are relatively comfortable and the collateral requirement isn't difficult either. Again, credit score is important. Make sure your taxes are filed annually, confirm employment if there's been employment, and take care of all the other crossings of t's and dotting of i's. They look at the risk factors, they score it, and then they price it. It's simpler than going to the bank and faster. There's very much a market for them today.

To find them, go online or pick up a copy of *Inc.* or *Entrepreneur*—they usually advertise there. You can also search online for "small business loans." You can then spend the whole night getting applications ready for free. They'll usually get back to you within twenty-four hours. You're not dealing with loan sharks; you're just dealing with a higher interest rate, because they're balancing the risk and reward. If your bank will loan to you at 6 percent, these companies may charge 15 percent. You may not care if you're in a startup situation or you know you can pay the loan back quickly. These loans aren't ideal for an acquisition, but they can be great for working capital once you acquire the company. It's all relative.

The activity in small business loans in the internet marketplace is very large. The banks now have such a difficult time lending because of government regulation and compliance and a huge market has opened for the underserved small business buyer.

SOURCES OF EQUITY

In addition to coming from you and your family, friends,

and assorted fools, equity can come from professional sources.

When private equity participates in a buyout, they're looking for a very specific situation. They have cash and expertise in particular industries. For them to do a deal, it needs to be the right size, the right industry, the right vertical, and with the right long-term strategy for how things are going to unfold. You're not going to bring a small company to a private equity firm. They don't work that way. Private equity lenders are more like partners, so you need to be doing a good-sized internal deal to bring them in.

A private equity firm will want to see you actively managing the company and they're going to be actively concerned with what you're doing. From a financial and strategic standpoint, they're very involved.

The great thing about private equity is they're always looking for deals. We get calls all the time. If you're on your own, you can approach them directly. The Association for Corporate Growth is an association for venture capitalist and private equity firms that you can connect with, and certainly a web search will turn up plenty of equity groups. If you're looking for money, bankers certainly have these relationships as well.

INDIVIDUAL INVESTORS

Private equity firms are institutionalized. They have a dedicated source of capital that goes to single investors. Individual investors, sometimes called angel investors, are usually individuals or a group of individuals looking to get involved by investing in a company. They're generally high net worth individuals who are willing to take a chance on an investment. They often come into startups looking to raise capital and will take an equity stake in the company but are known to invest in established businesses as well.

These investors actually market themselves. You might be able to find them online, but usually an individual investor will come through a referral from your attorney, your accountant, or your financial advisor. Sometimes they work in a formalized structure with the referral source, other times it's informal. Exploit your business and personal networks to find individual investors interested in your industry.

MEZZANINE INVESTORS

Mezzanine investors are a sort of hybrid of equity investors and debt financing. They're investment groups that have large access to capital. Mezzanine is like the Wild West of financing, because the investment can be structured however the groups want. It's essentially equity-like money, without giving up the equity. Mezzanine investors typically come in on larger deals, but there are some funds out there that will do a smaller deal. A smaller deal for them is a couple of million dollars. They can be an effective way to fill a financing gap.

Mezzanine investors used to be involved in the investment for just a short time, but today most mezzanine investors are involved for five to seven years on average. They get rewarded financially, because they're filling in a gap. They take a lot of risk, which is why you'll pay a high interest rate to work with them. You want to fill in your gap, make money, and get them their money back as soon as possible.

Why do they call it mezzanine? It's at a different level—up from the good seats. If you take their money, you're typically looking at annual returns in excess of 20 percent on the overall investment. The interest rate may not be bad, but they might structure a payment as a royalty or have warrants as part of the transaction structure. The interest rate could be 5 to 7 percent, but then they want a 20 or 25 percent return on their capital when they get out. While it's expensive, mezzanine financing can be a great option for funding an acquisition and subsequent growth.

Mezzanine investors are ideal for situations that are going to be growth-oriented and where there's a gap in the initial financing. You need equity-like funding, but you don't want to give up equity. These investors also prefer larger deals, but some do participate in smaller transactions. You may need to do some research to find groups interested in your deal.

THE DEVIL IS IN THE DETAILS

There are a lot of complexities to getting financing for a good deal. It's not inexpensive, and there are a lot of avenues to explore. Understand the covenants on what you're signing up for. Remember, the devil is in the details.

The most important part of the financing puzzle is preparation. You'll need solid documentation, such as your business plan, financial projections, and due diligence findings to get over the hurdles that the bank and other financers will present. Make sure your projections are realistic. Unfortunately, we've seen some projections that banks have funded on that don't indicate the buyer's future success. They're unrealistic, but the bank says, "OK, we got a checkbox on it, great." They're not going to tell you if it's a bad deal. The deal works for them, for what they can get out of it, and they want it.

BACKUP PLANS

While it's hard to imagine while you're in the midst of working through the details, it's important to have a plan B and a plan C if you're far into the deal. If things start to fall apart with other conventional sources of financing, the seller is the financer of last resort. What frustrates many sellers, though, is that they usually want cash on exit. If they're financing the transaction, that's unlikely to occur. They're taking more risk.

If the financing becomes a real challenge, you may need to restructure the deal. In this case, sometimes the seller takes on more financing, changes the terms of the deal, or says, "Go get more money and come back when you're ready." They may also increase the price to account for their additional risk. It all depends on how motivated the seller is.

In some of these deals, the money up front isn't that big a deal in the overall scheme of things. It shouldn't be driving the situation, yet it is. However, the buyer needs to keep in mind the seller's obligations upon an exit. They have debts to pay off, advisors to pay, and taxes to pay. You must be cognizant of all that during the process.

At some point, you may have to say, "Listen, this is not working. I'm going to walk away." You realize the deal just can't be financed, considering the buyer's and seller's realities. That's when the pushback starts. Most agreements have financing contingencies in them. You have a period of time in which you have to get your financing. Then you can ask for an extension. If you get one extension, you might get another, but usually by the second time you ask for an extension, if you don't have the financing, it's not on its way. That's when you say, "OK, I tried." It happens more than we'd like.

The bank can also show up with a last-minute change in what they're willing to give you. They say, "No, we changed our mind. We went to the loan committee on this and now this is what we're thinking." This puts you in a tough bind. They get greedy. It's the Golden Rule—they have the gold.

With your financing in place, it's time to close.

12

GET TO CLOSE

For a deal to close, it has to maintain a consistent flow. That can be challenging, because you're dealing with people and emotions. Deals are about control of the process. Depending on the situation, the control of the deal can swing between the buyer and the seller. Both have their challenges.

We've had buyers who are real grinders. They drag their feet constantly. They don't get back to the seller, or they tell the seller one thing and they do another. They're not truthful to the seller, and so the seller gets extremely aggravated. They get insulted. On the other end of the spectrum, there's the guy who has gone through the whole process and then makes a lowball offer, which angers the seller and pushes him away. We also have buyers who are out there looking to buy who don't push hard enough.

Sellers can also be a real pain to deal with if they constantly exercise their control. They can drag their feet on providing information. It's not uncommon for a seller to have an evolving thought process as to what they want. They're constantly moving the goal line as to what they want and what gets the deal done. Push too much and the buyer will walk away. Sometimes the best deals are the ones you don't do. A buyer has to learn when that's the case.

Anxiousness is a hallmark of any deal. Sellers are very anxious because they're selling. They want out and don't want to lose the deal. Buyers are less anxious for a plethora of reasons. Usually, when we're in the market to buy something, we're trained to take our time and drag our feet a little bit and see if we can get a lower price or better terms or find things in due diligence that are going to work on our behalf. This can certainly tire a seller out. If a buyer drags it out too long or thinks they have too much control because of where they are in the process, a smart seller will walk away. Once a seller recognizes that they don't need to sell, a buyer's ability to control the deal by creating anxiousness in the seller is lost. As a buyer, you have to be wary of tiring a seller out.

How do you know if you're pushing a seller too hard? With our years of experience, we've developed a good instinct for knowing boundaries. Everyone wants to negotiate and find the win-win. Everyone's got to win something. Buyers are driven toward that frame of mind.

If you nickel and dime your seller enough, your seller's going to tell you, "See you later. I'm done. I'll start over again. Get the hell out of here!" It becomes too adversarial. It's as though someone's coming to look at your house. They know the price; it's on the market. But they constantly keep coming back and finding reasons for why they don't want to buy it. They just keep torturing you, asking you to keep lowering your price because your Realtor wants you to sell. Eventually, you say, "I'm not selling it for that. See you later."

If you have good business instincts, you can feel when you're losing the deal. Remember, the seller might have two or three other buyers lined up as their own plan B. Even if the seller agrees with the buyer, someone else might be looking as well. As a buyer, you need to keep this in mind. If your seller is smart, they have at least one backup plan.

If it gets to the point where the seller doesn't like you, they're going to be more concerned with the principle of the deal than the money. Sellers get tired of difficult buyers. We had one deal where the buyer and seller could barely stand to be in the same room. It didn't start that way, as our buyer was a longtime employee, but that's where it ended up. They were threatening to sue each other before the deal was closed. This is not where you want a transaction to go, particularly one that involves a family member or a longtime boss.

You don't have to be best buddies, but you don't want to be antagonists either. If it gets to be antagonistic, the seller is probably going to tell you to go somewhere else. Even if you can't stand to look at them anymore, you need to stay friendly and on good terms during the acquisition period, even during tough negotiations, to make the deal happen. Closing and post-closing, they don't have to be your friend, but during the acquisition period, you need to keep the relationship on solid ground.

Humans are unpredictable, and people pick up on all sorts of strange things. You may be negotiating with someone for weeks and you might be hanging out with them at a conference when they say, "I don't like my grandchildren." All of a sudden, your entire perception of that person has changed. If you're a dog lover and someone said, "The last dog I had, I put him down because I didn't like him," that would affect you. We hear tons of things that make us think, "Really?" They can affect how the parties feel about going forward with the negotiations.

GOING DARK

Communication can be tricky, and it can be telling. When communications break down and the deal goes dark, you know you're on thin ice. A buyer and seller may have been chasing each other around for a week, and then it goes dark for a few days. That's when the nerves start to tingle.

Going dark frequently means someone's trying to find a way out. Someone's not happy. Either the buyer wants to get out, and the seller's calling us every five minutes, or the seller wants to get away from the buyer.

We have prospective buyers and sellers ghost us all the time. They'll just stop calling. They start out interested, we have meetings, we have LOI discussions, and then they just go dark. This isn't good practice and it definitely can't happen with an internal transaction. The risks of not being transparent and open in communication are too great.

When going dark happens, you have to do your best to hold the deal together. We try to get to the bottom of it. Sometimes the principals need to go into a little cooling off period. We encourage them to get back in there. If it's bad news, you might as well deal with the bad news right away.

THE THRESHOLD ON BOTH SIDES

If someone says, "$500,000 and not a penny less," sometimes they mean it and sometimes they don't. We have some sellers who hold the line, but generally, we tend to believe there's some flexibility. If the seller is open to negotiation, you should be practical in deciding how hard to push the outer limit. The offer should always make sense for both sides. Your counteroffer or your first offer shouldn't insult anyone—make sure it's within the parameter of reason. When a seller says, "I need $50,000," it doesn't mean he wouldn't sell for $40,000 if it was the right deal, if it was quick enough, and so on. If he says to you, "I have to net $50,000, I have no choice; I have bills to pay," then you know you have to offer more than $50,000. A lot of sellers tell us that as long as they get their net, they don't care much about the details of the deal.

EMOTIONS RUNNING HIGH

Getting to close is like getting married. Unfortunately, sometimes you get left at the altar. And it can be hard to anticipate that. Does it happen the morning of the closing? The day before the closing? Six weeks before the closing? You can get to the very last minute and it still falls apart. Over the years, we've learned that you never count on the deal until the papers are signed and the checks exchanged.

RELY ON COUNSEL—TO A DEGREE

Listen to your instincts along with your counselors. You've got good advisors and you should trust them, but if something's telling you this isn't a good deal, walk away. Go with your gut.

We see buyers getting cold feet because they get overwhelmed with the risk or the changes in their lifestyle or the money at stake, or because they feel they're in too far. Buyers are taking a step into the unknown, and in the end, for some it's too much. When something doesn't feel right, it makes more sense to take a step back than to leap in.

WHY ARE YOU AT THE TABLE?

Why are you at the table, doing this deal? You're there to buy the business or you're there to sell the business. Sometimes we lose sight of that. As an insider buyer, you must stay focused on that reason. You can't get yourself caught up in the minutiae going on day to day in the business. Stay focused. Let your advisors work through all the nonsense. You'll likely get to a point in the deal when you need to remind yourself why the deal seemed like a great idea to begin with. Look at the bigger picture.

DEAL FATIGUE

Deal fatigue sets in when things drag on so long that everything feels like it's stuck in an interminable process. When this happens, we try to speed it up. We might call for a sit- down and say, "All right, how do we get this on track? We're going a little bit slow here."

Push it forward. That's always the key. You've got to always be pushing forward, otherwise you'll never get to the close.

You'll always need to push the accountants and the lawyers. They have a tendency to get bogged down in the details and process. Plus, some advisors see the value in negotiating every minor detail like it's a big one—in their mind, it demonstrates their value and increases the bill. You must be an advocate for your own deal and be able to communicate what is important and what is not.

You can use the due diligence time limits to push things forward, because you usually have a certain time period to get it done. If you stay on that clock and work hard to get your due diligence completed, you'll keep the momentum moving. Ask questions, keep moving forward, push everyone else forward, too: "Let's go, let's go, let's go!"

LEVERAGE YOUR RELATIONSHIP WITH THE SELLER

If you've built a relationship with the seller, leverage it. If the seller likes baseball, make sure you learn enough about baseball to talk about it. Leverage what you know. And don't be afraid to step away from the table. Talk about the deal somewhere else, or step away completely and say, "I'm tired. I need some time to think." And go. It's good for the deal. Once you've done your thinking, if you still want to buy, come back in and start over again.

We often have what are called sidebar conversations. If

things bog down or get heated, we'll take clients out of the room for a few minutes so everyone can cool off and get some perspective. When we come back in, we can reconnect and move the negotiation forward.

Sometimes it's best for the buyer and seller to be one-on-one. It's best if they say, "You know, I respect your advisors and I respect mine, but it's time for both of us to sit down and talk." At that point, you can look each other in the eye and have a candid conversation. Nine times out of ten, the issues are resolved.

SELLER ENTITLEMENT

The seller usually feels that he's doing right by the buyer in selling them the company. But the seller usually feels that the buyer's not doing him a big enough favor. We try to get them to meet in the middle, but you do need to know when to walk away.

Buyers need to know their own threshold. At what point does the deal-making become detrimental? We do our best to meet in the middle between each side's feelings of entitlement and sometimes greed, but you need to know when to walk away. You can overtalk the deal and overthink it, and we can overfacilitate it.

If you do walk away, you're probably walking away forever.

SUNK COSTS

As a buyer, you could know it's a bad deal, but still you think, "Geez, I've already put so much time and money into this." Buyers have trouble walking away. It's not just all the time and money they've spent; it's also the treasure. Treasure refers to how expensive it is today to be in deals. How many people get locked in and move forward because they don't want to let go of the money?

No one likes to go out as a loser either. You don't want to go home at the end of the day and get asked how the deal went only to say, "We walked away. We couldn't get our own way." It's like breaking up. Who breaks up with whom? Do you say, "It's me, not you?"

If a buyer understands that the deal is a gamble, it's not going to be too hard for them to walk away. They're going to be able to justify it by saying $10,000 was easy to lose versus the risk they were just about to acquire. You're always a little bitter, however, when you put money in and it doesn't turn out. You feel sick inside, but there also comes a time when you realize that you just can't go through with it, the deal just doesn't make sense. You thought it did, for weeks, and then suddenly it doesn't. Sometimes the best deals are the ones that don't get done.

You've made your deal. Everybody's reasonably happy.

Your needs are mostly being met. The seller's needs are mostly being met. Now it's time for the transition.

13

THE TRANSITION PLAN

We were involved in the acquisition of an eye doctor's practice. The new owner was dead set on switching the practice over to electronic health records immediately after taking over. Medicare and Medicaid mandate electronic health records, but it's not mandated that you have to go in and change everything on the first day. He was so aggressive about it that several of the other doctors left and took their patients with them—the change was too much too soon for them.

New owners tend to be very gung-ho. They're so eager to do things their way that they sometimes make very rash decisions about starting new initiatives. In the case of the eye doctors, the new owner forcing change meant that all the key employees moved on quickly. There was no practice left.

You have to have a plan for what happens after you close.

But even if you have the best plan, you've got to make sure that it culturally fits the new acquisition.

IF IT AIN'T BROKE, DON'T FIX IT

We advise our clients that as much as you want to make changes immediately, if the business wasn't failing when you bought it, it doesn't need to be fixed immediately. Of course, you can see things that need to change, but take time to observe and get a sense of the company's personalities and how the operation works. Even an insider with intimate knowledge of the company needs to observe from the ownership seat for a while to appreciate the full picture. Only then, implement the changes that are going to be the least painful. Focus on the low-hanging fruit that can yield benefits and build goodwill with employees.

Everyone hates change, employees especially. The number one thing that always concerns employees when a business gets sold is, what's going to happen to me? How is this going to affect my job? Am I going to get fired? Am I going to like my boss? If you create change too fast, you can end up with a rebellion on your hands.

In the movie *The Patriot*, Mel Gibson says to his son when preparing to ambush the British soldiers, "Aim small, miss small." That's a great approach to transitioning. Figure out the easy things that aren't going to be that disruptive and start with those. With the small simple things, if you miss on them, fine. They don't cause chaos or serious disruption. Make small changes, such as adding a weekly staff meeting or tweaking hours a bit or getting new desk chairs for everybody.

A great example is one of our clients, who acquired a business that had a lot of challenges. The first thing he did, though, was paint and upgrade the office and start making other investments in the facility. This was huge for the employees, because they saw him as committed to changes that were to their benefit. Later, when he started making bigger changes, the employees trusted him and got on board.

We think it's also very important that you have a written plan put together that lays out what's going to happen week one, week two, week three, and so on from there. Identify the things you want to start to transition and the things you want to put into play. Over the first six weeks, we recommend starting to interview everyone to get a sense for what they do and to discover their concerns about the business or the company.

LISTEN TO THE BUSINESS

Get the employees to speak to you by being very observant and asking the right questions. It's like anything else;

ask very open-ended questions to allow them to explain. Spend some time with them one-on-one and share ideas. It's like any good job interview: you're doing well as the candidate when you're not speaking. If you listen, you'll hear that the company is telling you all sorts of things. You've got to talk to as many people as possible before you make any decisions or comments.

Do the same thing with the customers. Visit your customers in person, introduce yourself. There's nothing like the personal touch. You can learn a ton about what they think of your company.

We often get engaged to do an assessment of the business, understanding its competencies, infrastructure, and inherent challenges. We assess where the business is from a people standpoint. Where are the gaps? What is the direction of the company? What does the culture look like? Where are processes and systems in place? Is there uniformity? What's broken or dysfunctional? Sometimes an employee won't talk to the boss or the new owner about concerns, but they will talk to a stranger. It's amazing how much they open up. We're objective and they know they can trust us to be discreet.

For these interviews, we use a variety of different assessment tools. We have a set of questions that we've developed on how we assess and look at a company. We pull from a database of more than two hundred different questions. We might ask someone, "Besides the owners, can you identify who the leaders in the organization are?" We ask this to find out who the informal leaders are, because sometimes it's not the people you think. We might get comments such as, "There are no leaders in our organization."

We may also ask, "What do you see as the company's strengths or weaknesses?" or, "If there was one thing about the way the company does business, what would you change?" You can see why, if you were the owner, you would get someone else to ask that question. What if someone in the company was asking the question and the answer was get rid of you?

Based on this, we help the new owner identify the issues and help them figure out what the solutions are. We make recommendations on what we think they need to do. A lot of the times, it comes down to putting an operating system in place for how the business is going to run and how to create the discipline to run it.

We are big fans of the work of Jim Collins, author of *Good to Great*. His analysis and insights into what makes companies successful and why they fail is the foundation of our approach to advising our clients in creating value. There are several great approaches that allow clients to turn the work of Collins into an actionable framework for operating their companies. A couple worth checking out are the concepts detailed in *Mastering the Rockefeller Habits* and *Scaling Up,* both by Verne Harnish.

We help our clients implement an operating system called the Entrepreneurial Operating System (EOS), which is based on the book *Traction: Get a Grip on Your Business,* by Gino Wickman. Our clients use it to get their employee buy-in, build their strategy and alignment, and get things done. It's all very commonsense stuff, but it works. You can't always think of all these things on your own. Other sources that are worth checking out are *The E-Myth,* by Michael Gerber and *The 4 Disciplines of Execution,* by Sean Covey.

LISTEN TO THE CULTURE

You pay attention to the business's existing culture because if you don't have good people, you can't build a successful and sustainable business. We don't care how great your product is or your service or anything else, if you don't have your people aligned to your values and vision and accountable for performance, it's not going to work. Without good people who are committed to your values and creating a culture that people want to be a part of, then you don't have a good business.

We see businesses fail all the time because of bad culture. Bad culture sabotages a business. If you have people teaming up against the culture all the time, splitting off into camps or making political alliances or forming little cliques, you have a bad culture. What organization hasn't gone through those problems at some point? To mitigate and eradicate a bad culture, you need to replace it with a good culture throughout the entire system that everyone buys into and understands.

THE LINGERING SELLER

As the new owner, you want to make the company your own. You want to show an appropriate respect for the past, particularly because you were part of it. You also need to keep the past and the ghost of the seller in perspective. If the past owner was well respected and admired, there is probably a lot of reverence for them. Obviously, they were able to build up the company and create a business that had enough value that you wanted to buy it. At the same time, they probably did a lot of things wrong. As the new owner, you have to fix a lot of things that are broken and change things to get the organization moving to where you want it to go.

As a new owner, you're excited to get started. It becomes easy to try to do too many things at once. Patience is a virtue, and that's particularly true when it comes to implementing change in an established business and culture. You need to understand the nature of the company and not try to make too many changes too quickly. A lot of entrepreneurs will start up a company and then, when it gets down to the daily grind of just running it, they're not interested anymore. The new owners come in and then all that startup excitement just turns into routine. It's very hard to transition from entrepreneur to seasoned owner. Some of that great, exciting culture that was instilled as an entrepreneur gets watered down and wastes away. It has to be reexamined and reinvented all the time.

MAKE A LIST, BUILD A TEAM

Formulate the transition plan as early as possible. We recommend getting a start on it while you're doing your due diligence. During that time, you're uncovering things and you're thinking clearly. Start putting together a running list. Of course, you want to keep it quiet; your seller doesn't need to know what you're thinking.

Your transition team is primarily made up of the advisors you've been working with. You might include some new sets of eyes and ears, such as someone you have in mind for a role in the company. You may need to bring in others, such as HR specialists, strategists, and marketing experts. It all depends on how happy you are with the company's approach to these areas.

You also need to determine who's on your team internally. Sometimes the people you're dealing with during the transaction, the insiders who are talking the most and selling the most, are the last people you want once you get inside the door. You need to protect yourself from the busybodies. There's always a queen bee inside the office. There are always a couple of guys in the shop who control every bit of information. Those are the people you watch out for. Those who know the most are probably also the least credible and might not be too popular among their colleagues. But employees also look to these people because they're the ones with the information.

As power changes in an organization, people change camps. Some were overlooked by the previous management and will now have a chance to shine. Some will form a clique that opposes you and will need to be let go or will quit on their own, saving you the trouble.

WORK WITH WHAT YOU HAVE

Long term, some people in the organization might not be the people you want as far as their skill set or core values. They've been with the old company a while, however, so you have to deal with them. You're better off for doing it. Engage with them and let them fail or fix themselves. In a lot of the organizations we deal with, there's a definite lack of management and leadership talent when we come in. We come in and say, "You need to think about the business strategically now. We want to do X, Y, and Z to improve the business." If you're the new owner and you're looking to do these things, you should realize you can't do them on your own. Evaluate the talent pool around you. Identify what you have here and how you can work with them so that you can start to make progress until you can get the people you want. You always start with a certain amount of deadwood left from the previous owner.

When we start our facilitation with the Traction process, one of the first things we'll tell the group is, "Just because you're here at the table today doesn't mean you're going to be here at the table tomorrow. You have to earn that place." Sometimes the talent pool within the company is just too shallow. No matter how much you'd like to keep everybody on, you're going to have to look beyond the current employees.

BUILD ALLIANCES WITH THE RIGHT PEOPLE

Watch out for the person who helps with the acquisition and tells you everything that's wrong. That person is not your ally here. They're trying to protect themselves, so they're trying to build their own powerbase. The way they do this is by making themselves indispensable. Then it's easier for them to stick the knife in your back.

If you find people genuinely willing to help and you can

give them the tools to be successful, it's going to pay off well for you. Of course, you would want to do that for everybody. It's just some people are going to take advantage of it more. A lot of times, an employee might not yet have had a role of great responsibility, but you know they're going to be a rock star if you put them on your management team.

Look for the potential. For the old hands in the company, the transition may not be favorable, but for the ones who weren't in a favored position, the transition is promising. It gives them opportunity. We've seen many a neglected employee become a star under the guidance of a new owner.

YOU'RE THE NEW OWNER. CONGRATULATIONS! YOU'RE SCREWED

The downside of buying a business is you're also buying its baggage. You're buying lots of good things, but you're also buying the bad things that come with them. If you have a bad culture, if you have bad business processes, if you have bad customers, or bad pricing or any number of bad other things, it's going to take a lot of work to fix. Now you own it. It can take years to change an organization and get it to where you want it to be. It's a long process because you're dealing with people and there are often a lot of sacred cows.

You might have an employee who's very productive, but every Tuesday she has a blowup that causes complete chaos. You might want to fire her, but you have to look at the ramifications of doing that. There's only so much short-term pain that you can allow yourself to incur. It might be better to just deal with her for now. That's why you're screwed. You're saying, "I bought this business because of the potential it has, because there's a good foundation here. To get it there, I know need to do a lot of different things." It takes a lot of time to turn a battleship around.

14

EXPECT LEGACY COSTS

Legacy costs are the unexpected costs of the transaction that remain after the deal is done. You thought what you paid for the company was the cost, but then you didn't realize the extent of the hidden costs. You're potentially going to be paying these for a long time. Inside buyers generally have a better handle on the legacy costs they're inheriting, but most of our clients are amazed at the depth of these costs and what it takes to eliminate them.

Legacy costs can be hard to quantify because they're unknown until you hit them. We've had instances where there are employees who really shouldn't be employees anymore, but because of their relationship with another employee, they're kept on. For instance, we had a mother and a son situation in which the son was a highly valued resource and very marketable and the mother was just a disaster. Our client needed to move the mother out, but that meant potentially losing a key employee.

In a situation like that, the best thing is to negotiate. The negotiation may cause hard feelings, especially if family members are involved. We had a situation in a family business where the father tried to balance the ledger between his children. The son bought the business. But there was also a side venture that the father and son had set up. The father gave our buyer's sister 25 percent of that entity, even though she wasn't involved with it. The sister added no value and our client wanted to buy out her interest. They've had it valued, but the sister put a very unreasonable price on her share. It's a brutal legacy cost. It will cost hundreds of thousands of dollars for her to leave—a cost that could have been avoided.

Deathbed legacies can come into play in partnerships and family businesses. We had a client in his thirties who had an older partner. They did a startup together and the business grew. They became good friends and fifty-fifty partners. Then the older partner was diagnosed with cancer and deteriorated rapidly. His lifetime girlfriend was in the business on payroll, but she didn't do anything. He loved her very much and he wanted her to be taken care of.

Because he was so emotionally attached to the business and his friend and willing to do whatever he could to keep his business going, the young partner promised the old partner that he would take care of the girlfriend. Over the years, he became more and more resentful and bitter as he watched her staying on payroll and not doing anything for it. Eventually, that legacy promise, that "I will always make sure she's OK," came to a head. We had to resolve it legally. She had to be notified she was going off payroll.

It was traumatic. He kept her on another year. Then she had a health crisis. She wasn't old enough to go on Medicare yet, so he felt he had to keep her on payroll and the company health insurance. It was a sad situation, but that's what an emotional legacy costs.

Legacies of that sort don't come up in due diligence. They come up after you close the deal, and you have to make a decision about what to do. Employees have all sorts of side deals about hours, flextime, and the like. Accommodations are important, but some side deals are for recruiting and retaining employees. You might decide no one's working from home anymore. Then a key employee says, "Oh yeah?" You might need to rethink the work-from-home decision. Employee satisfaction isn't only about raises anymore, though that's always an issue. It's about quality of life and flexibility. As the new owner, you want your own quality of life to be good. Your employees want the same thing.

Another type of very challenging legacy cost is the retention of advisors. The seller may require you to use their advisors as part of the deal—they want to make sure their interests are protected. When an advisor isn't someone you chose, you don't have the relationship the previous owner did. You're always wary about who's interest they're really working for. The flip side of this is that if the seller has trusted advisors in place, it's very beneficial for you to try and build relationships with them. They can be a voice of reason you can rely on when handling post-deal issues with the seller.

YOU CAN'T FIX EVERYTHING

The area where we see the biggest legacy costs is in the people side of the business. These are challenging issues to fix, and sometimes you can't fix them in the time or manner that you want. You may have some employee issues that can't be fixed at all. That legacy employee who for whatever reason can't be let go? You may just have to wait for that person to move on, or retire, or die.

We spend a lot of our post-transaction work with our clients advising on changing the culture. New owners want a culture that reflects their personalities and core values. Fixing culture is a long process. The root of many culture issues can usually be pinpointed to a couple of employees. Once you figure out who the ringleaders are, you're going to have to find a way to mitigate their influence or move them out, as painful as it may be. You might not be able to do it as quickly as you want, particularly if you're a small company.

There is a balancing act to dealing with these legacy problem people. If someone has a lot of authority and you minimize that authority because you don't want them to have it anymore, that person is not going to go quietly. If you're taking something away from someone, especially if it's visible, you've got to be prepared to replace them or battle them.

Legacy employees are valuable on many levels, but the disruption they can cause in the culture is problematic. It's very hard to go backward, but it happens to lots of longtime employees during a transition. An employee may be a top dog in the company because of their relationship with the owner, but they're in a position of responsibility where they shouldn't be. They frequently recognize that, so they do what they can to impede the transition for the new owner. As the new owner, how you deal with these people is going to be critical to your success. Their influence needs to be minimized but in a manner that doesn't rock the boat and create even larger issues for you.

We once had a client who acquired a company and quickly found out that the president was in way over his head. Worse, he was a cultural nightmare, as his particular strength was in solving the problems he created. Despite this, he had significant knowledge and talents that were beneficial to the organization and weren't easily replaced. The approach we took with our client was to gradually remove responsibilities from him until we had him in the seat on the bus where he belonged. By focusing on what he was good at, he became happier and an asset for the company.

Each ownership transition is unique because each company and situation is unique. There's no template. As an insider, you have the benefit of familiarity, so you have a clearer sense of what needs to be done. At the same time, that familiarity makes it hard to make changes, because the employees know you as well. You're a known commodity and you don't have the mystique that an outsider might have.

How you go about that transition and dealing with your legacy employees is a decision you need to make in advance of buying the company. You may decide that on day one you need to just walk in and fire somebody, because that's a great way to send a message that there is a change in management. Our preference is to create buy-in and accountability from all employees. One of the easiest ways to implement the transition is to hire an expert from the outside to help.

Ultimately, cultural change in an organization is about

creating a system of accountability. If someone decides they want to keep their job, you need to be clear about how to do that. If you create that accountability, people are either going to fall in line or they're not.

Legacy costs are just part of doing business; you have them no matter what. They're inevitable because people aren't machines. They have feelings and relationships.

BE THE BEST TYPE OF OWNER

Let's say you've got a restaurant business with a great bartender. When that bartender works, your place is jamming. You say, "This is great. Everyone loves Freddy. What a great bartender." Why does everyone love Freddy? Because it turns out Freddy is giving away shots. He's not ringing in drinks. He's giving away the place because it's driving his tips upward. What you realize is Freddy isn't really a good bartender for you. He's not actually bringing in customers; he's leveraging and taking advantage of the system to benefit himself. What happens? Is there a way to go about getting rid of him?

You can confront Freddy. He's going to deny it, and you have no proof. Instead, you can create a process and accountability system so that it doesn't happen anymore. Technology today can track every pour and every drink that gets served. Freddy now has a choice. He can either get on board and follow the system or he can leave. It becomes his decision, rather than you giving him an ultimatum. The best owners are ones who know how to create accountability in an organization.

Accountability also is the confidence that you're going to do what you say you're going to do. If you say, "I'm going to give you the tools and the resources to do your job and not worry about you doing it," you have to do it. If you give your employees the tools and resources, then they're accountable.

You can prepare all you want—there will still be some hidden legacy costs. You just don't know what they are yet. Ups and downs are to be expected. Now, it's time to build value for the future.

(15)

VALUE BUILDING

What happens when a new owner doesn't set up processes to ensure future success? We represented a large corporate client in a substantial deal. They did due diligence and spent a lot of money to ensure that the earnings were there, that the employees were there, and that the customers were there. They did, very professionally, everything you would expect them to do.

They spent so much effort on making sure they got a good deal that they overlooked the most important thing: understanding the business. Although they had eighty companies in their portfolio, this one was a new area for them. They didn't look past the day of the closing to think about whether the acquisition was a good fit and what its future would be. They didn't plan for how they would build value in their new property. They started losing good employees, including a controller who was really good at what she did, and couldn't hire good replacements.

The deal looked good on paper when they closed, but three years later it was worth only half of what they paid.

LIFELONG LEARNING

Value building is a very hot topic these days. Everyone wants to build companies that scale. They want to know how to take a business that's doing X, take it to Y, and sell it for Z.

Value building can be tricky. Operating systems, such as Traction and Rockefeller, provide principles that companies can utilize. You can also sit down with a coach and work on solving problems, improving yourself, and building your skills.

We believe there are also commonsense business practices that need to be retaught all the time. At the end of the day, business is simple. We suggest finding a good business advisor who can take you through some very simple and practical methods of doing business based on tried-and-true experience.

Remembering the basics can be hard when you've just acquired a business and you're moving ahead with your new ideas at full speed. Sometimes you have to do more by doing less. Slow down and focus.

DEALING WITH MEETINGS

One of the biggest challenges new owners face is dealing with meetings. We find there are very few companies that do meetings right. Some have no formalized meeting structure in place, so trying to create a culture where meetings occur on a frequent basis can be hard. You need discipline to set aside a time for regular meetings on the calendar. There's always something more important than the meeting.

Bad habits are hard to break, so dealing with companies that have random or infrequent meetings can be painful. Companies that have meetings inherently think they are doing it right because they are meeting—as if the fact of the meeting is a victory in and of itself. At the same time, employees probably dread the meeting, because it's long, repetitive, and often nothing more than a reporting or bitch session.

Good meetings have a consistency and flow to them that quickly communicates what needs to be reported, while maximizing the time for discussion and engagement. Our clients who "get it" implement a range of different meetings that include daily, weekly, quarterly, and annual meetings.

The huddle is an example of a daily meeting that is highly effective and efficient. The huddle is at the same time every day and is focused on communicating the most important things that are going to occur over the next day. They move quickly and get everyone aligned and prioritized. A quick web search of "daily huddle" will bring you to videos of great examples of how a company runs a daily huddle.

The weekly meeting is focused on the business of the business. In Traction/EOS, it's known as the Level 10 meeting. It follows a very specific agenda and occurs every week at the same time and date. Attendance is mandatory. The meeting runs for ninety minutes, with the bulk of the time geared toward issue solving.

As easy as they sound, it takes a tremendous amount of discipline to master these daily and weekly meetings. The benefits of doing so are massive—you actually focus on the issues of the business, rather than the day-to-day crises that pop up.

Quarterly and annual meetings are a great way to get your team refocused. We recommend to our clients that they have a daylong offsite meeting every quarter and a two-day offsite meeting once a year. The purpose is to review and refresh the business strategy and tackle the really big issues. Offsite meetings are also really great for team building, as there's nothing like having everyone out of the office and away from the formalities that requires.

THOUGHT, ACTION, SUCCESS

Organizations that have disciplined people with disciplined thought and who take disciplined actions will result in success. If you're not committed to it, then you can't make the time. We know it's hard. We don't have a single business, ours included, where we're not overwhelmed a lot of the time. It's easy to not focus on those things that you should be doing to move forward. Are there other things we could do in those three hours today? Yeah, we can find a million of them, but it's important to our big picture; that's why we're there. If it's important, you find the time, or you make the time.

TALK TO US

When you're buying out the boss, knowledge is half the battle. The other half is getting the right people to help you. You'll probably buy a business only once or twice in your lifetime—get experienced people who do this all the time to help you make the best deal you can.

The Vann Group focuses on helping you be a better businessperson. We love helping our clients take the next step in their business development. We love to see employees become bosses and go on to build and improve their companies. We're a multigenerational, family-owned firm—we understand the issues involved with intergenerational company transfers and selling a small to mid-market company. We provide the advice, guidance, and execution capabilities that owners and buyers need to create, maximize, and realize the unlocked value of a business.

To discuss the future of your business, please contact us. We're here to help.

Vann Group
819 Worcester Street
Springfield, MA 01151
Ten Post Office Square, 8th floor
Boston, MA 02109
info@vann-group.com
(413) 543-2776
www.vann-group.com
www.buyingouttheboss.com

ABOUT THE AUTHORS

KEVIN VANN and his son **MICHAEL VANN** are principals in the Vann Group, a firm that has helped business owners with succession planning since 1979. Over the years, the Vanns have guided hundreds of business leaders through the transfer of ownership, providing both buy-side and sell-side representation while ensuring the continued success of the companies. The succession and transition plans that they assist in developing incorporate the entire spectrum of decisions about finances, taxes, operations, and leadership.

Made in the USA
Middletown, DE
31 October 2019